AF601776

# MY GRANDMOTHER'S LETTERS FROM AMSTERDAM

Bertha and Hanna - August 1939

# MY GRANDMOTHER'S LETTERS FROM AMSTERDAM

RAYMOND KANN

First published in the UK in 2018 by
Raymond Kann Books, 30 Park Grove, Edgware, HA8 7SJ
raymondkann@gmail.com



ISBN 978-1-5272-1642-6



Designed and typeset by Pete Brown

Printed and bound by Lightning Source UK Ltd.

# CONTENTS

# PREFACE

AS I AM ABLE TO TRANSLATE THE LETTERS FROM Dutch into English I am writing this so that my children and their cousins, if they are interested, can have a glimpse into the world of their grandmother and great grandmother and into which I was born.

For many years a collection of old family papers passed from one brother to another until David suggested that he keep them all together in one place. He kept them and made copies. He did this a few years ago and in due course I went through the copies and found correspondence from our grandmother in Amsterdam to our mother in London. This started about a week before the Second World War and continued for a few years. I arranged the letters chronologically and thought that even if they were read in the future the contents, which is in Dutch, would not be understood by my children. Almost everyone referred to has passed away over the last seventy years or so. Many cannot be identified. Where possible I have included notes to help recognise any relationships that might be known. You will soon get to know the main characters. In the then Dutch culture great store was set by the occasion of a birthday and a great fuss was made when these occurred, often being an excuse for a party or other form of celebration.

Almost every original letter is closely written to get as much news as possible onto each side of the sheet. When there was not enough room, or another thought needed recording, margins and any unwritten space was often used. To reflect this the format of the letters, most of which do not have paragraphs, are not right justified so as to reflect the originals.

Even if Bertha had wanted to tell her daughter the real truth of life under Nazi occupation this would not have been allowed. As soon as the war broke out all communications were subject to strict censorship by both the German and the English authorities. This naturally included the post and families could only connect by Red Cross message cards sent from one country to another. These messages were subject to long delays as they had to go via the Red Cross office in Geneva both on their way there and also when returned with a reply. The message could only consist of twenty five words, as could the reply. Post to or from neutral countries that in peacetime took a few days now took a matter of weeks, or longer, and was also the subject of delay by censorship. (Examples of typical postal examination are included towards the end of the story.)

There was another way of families communicating which was via a neutral country. A letter sent from England or the Netherlands to Switzerland was received there. The envelope was opened and the contents placed in an new envelope and forwarded to the recipient. This method allowed much more family news and chit chat to pass across borders and was also faster than the very limited Red Cross cards. But again the post from Switzerland was subject to the recipient country's censorship authorities. I expect that all the letters that we have were sent or received via this kind intermediary, a son of one of Bertha's friends, in Switzerland. It was with his help our mother and grandmother were able to communicate. His closing letter has been included.

To put into context the regulations introduced which specifically persecuted the Jewish population details of the measures imposed by the occupying Germans on the whole of Dutch society have also been included. This helps to show how all suffered under the increasingly severe restrictions imposed under the Nazi occupation. By the time of the extremely cold winter of 1944 Dutch people were so desperate for any kind of fuel they would even uproot trees from parks to burn in their grates, and were subsequently banned from access to all parks. The food shortage at that time was so extreme that the population was reduced to even eating or making soup out of tulip bulbs. The condition of the starving Dutch people was so bad that the Nazis allowed the neutral Swedes to make humanitarian food drops by parachute from Swedish aeroplanes so that the Dutch population at least had a little something to eat.

The dates quoted are based on a variety of sources which might sometimes conflict. Some may have used the original date the Order was made while others may quote the implementation date. If there are any errors or discrepancies please forgive me. Where relationships are known these have been shown as a footnote and are collected at the end. My thanks go to my son Michael not only for his help and advice but also ensuring that the project reached a conclusion.

# BACKGROUND

IT IS ALWAYS BEST TO START A STORY AT THE BEGINNING but in this case there are several strands stretching back over time. We have different stories that join together to relate what happened during the years around 1940. Europe had become a place of hatred, war and turmoil and the letters translated below reflect the hopes and fears of a very modest family basically struggling through life, like most people.

We need to go back over a couple of centuries to the villages and hamlets in the hills west of the river Rhine and south of Frankfurt where it seems that possibly a pedlar was making his regular rounds. He was a Jewish pedlar and it can be assumed that opportunity or romance played a part when he met a Jewish family whose daughter he married and decided to settle down in their small hamlet. The only known issue from the marriage of our pedlar and his wife was one son. This son is recorded as having seven children of whom five surprisingly, given the high rate of infant mortality, survived to adulthood. The same kind of pattern continued for the next few generations with the surviving children becoming Jewish brides and grooms and marrying into the Jewish families living in neighbouring villages. In each village there was a limited pool of suitable Jewish matches. Many of these new families' children might in turn marry back into the families living in the original village where their parents or grandparents may have lived.

By the middle of the nineteenth century western Europe was beginning to have the benefit of new railway lines which combined with increasing industrialisation led to the growth and expansion of towns. To service the new factories the population was attracted from the countryside to live in an urban environment. For the younger sons of a family who had mainly been involved in horse and cattle dealing for generations, with a few entering into retail butchery, the bright lights of opportunity in the towns were appealing. So over time several younger members left their traditional limited village life to settle down in the nearer industrial towns.

One of the young men who left his village as the 19th century turned to the 20th century was Simon Kann. He went to seek his fortune in a town called Duisburg. Duisburg is located at the confluence of the rivers Rhine and Ruhr and by that time was already becoming an area of heavy industry in Germany. Here he worked as a butcher and before the First World War managed to buy his own corner premises. This housed a shop, a small sausage factory and a few stables with living accommodation on the upper floors where he and his family lived. Simon and his wife Ida had three children, Grete, Hans and Erich. The whole family worked in the business.

Simon was a short and rather rotund person who died in 1931 at the age of 58. His wife Ida nominally continued to run the family business but it was in fact her two sons who did the work with the younger one taking the lead. (Hans had married Wilhelmina, always known as 'Wally' for short, in 1930 and they were blessed with a son Gunter in July 1936. In 1933 Grete married and moved to a town a short tram journey away with her only daughter Gisela arriving in 1935.)

Although there had always been anti-Semitism in Germany it had been at a relatively low key. Germany lost the First World War and the subsequent impossibly large reparation payments demanded by the victors led to political and financial instability culminating in hyper-inflation in 1923 and the subsequent recession. This created the discontent exploited by the National Socialist Party, inter alia, blaming the Jews for Germany losing the First World War despite many Jewish soldiers receiving medals while other Jews lost their lives fighting for the Fatherland, including one of Ida's brothers. The Nazi hatred of Communists was manifest by them physically attacking their meetings often achieving their intent of causing injury and worse on those attending. Economic conditions improved during the mid to late 1920s as a result of the stabilisation of the German currency. The 1929 Wall Street Crash spread financial failure and factory closures worldwide. This hit Germany even harder than most countries as the large amount of foreign credit used to rebuild its industry after the payment of the reduced war reparations was now suddenly withdrawn.

Germany became a country with a very high level of unemployment and poverty. The Nazi promises of employment for all helped to determine the outcome of the election on 30th January 1933 as Hitler came to power as Chancellor. The following year a referendum agreed that the office of the President and the Chancellor should be combined into one, effectively combining in one person the Head of State and the elected Prime Minister. Now that the Nazis were in control the beginning of legislation against the Jewish population was introduced. Over the following years further laws increasingly and systematically removed the Jewish population's civil and economic rights.

On the night of ninth November 1938 the SA paramilitaries (Nazis) unleashed a series of organised riots throughout Germany and Austria (which Germany had annexed in the March of that year) directed against the Jewish communities, burning down synagogues and violently attacking any Jews they found on the streets. In the space of a few hours, thousands of synagogues and homes were damaged or destroyed and many Jewish owned shops and businesses were vandalised. For the first time, tens of thousands of Jewish men were arrested and sent to concentration camps simply because they were Jewish. This included Hans and Erich who had never expressed any interest in politics. It was no longer a time to be a Jew in Germany.

By the end of January 1939 the brothers were released and it was obvious that the time had come to leave Germany but by then there were many bureaucratic obstacles in the way. Leaving Germany without going through the correct procedure, paying the assessed taxes meant virtually the confiscation of almost everything they possessed. The 'other' way was chosen and they quietly crossed the border into the Netherlands one evening, where they were caught by the Dutch police. As illegal immigrants they were promptly returned back to Germany and imprisoned in a local police station. Trying to escape from the Fatherland was a very serious matter.

While imprisoned as illegal emigrants in a German police station near the border a Nazi official approached Erich and asked if he was the butcher who used to sell meat in the marketplace in Duisburg. He admitted this and the official then replied that his mother, a poor First World War widow, had been one of his regular customers. This Nazi official now recalled that all the years his mother had been a customer she had always been given extra scraps or bones for her dog when she bought meat. She had no pets but the few bones from which she could make soup or small scraps of meat did help her to eke out her small pension. With this in mind he decided that there was no good reason to keep them in the police station any longer so the official told the two prisoners to go. Their mother must have been disappointed to see them home again so soon.

It was decided that another attempt to escape from Germany was to be made but this time they should finish up well away from the area near the border to somewhere the police would not be on the lookout for illegal immigrants. While plans were being made Hans was picked up and sent to a concentration camp just north of Berlin, Sachsenhausen, where he was sterilised. After a few weeks it was discovered that he had no political interests and was released.

As mentioned Duisburg is situated at the junction of the river Rhine and its tributary the river Ruhr. River barges carried the materials needed for the local heavy industry that then existed. A thriving international river trade stretching from the Dutch coastal ports down to Switzerland was carried out by barges transporting goods up and down waterways which continues to this very day. A captain of a barge was found who was willing to accept a large amount of money to smuggle Hans and Erich out of Germany downriver into the Netherlands. The evening before the barge was to set off the two men had to come aboard. They were shown their hiding place, a space between the outer and the inner hull, where the cargo as to be loaded. The next day the fully laden barge went downriver without incident and Hans and Erich were now in the Netherlands.

A picture of the barge in which the brothers left their not so beloved Fatherland

We now need to focus our attention on the city of Amsterdam whose golden age had long passed. As the Netherlands had not been at war since the time of Napoleon and had remained neutral during the First World War political events and conflicts elsewhere in Europe were not viewed as being a direct threat. The leadership of the City of Amsterdam decided in the early part of the twentieth century that it needed to expand the city in order to re-house those who lived in the city centre, an area of very poor decaying housing, slums and poverty. The inhabitants would be accommodated in new housing to be built on the arable land adjoining the south and west of the city. The new suburbs were built in the 1920s and 1930s. In one of these apartments in a district which is still called the 'New South' today we find the other unexpected characters of our story.

Bertha had nine siblings of which three died in infancy and none of whom were to survive the war. Bertha had married Abraham Crost at the then late age of twenty six and their only child, a daughter called Hanna, was born to Bertha a year after the wedding. When the girl was thirteen years old an event took place which, at the time, was one of great shame and embarrassment in a conservative society that still held on strongly to the conventions of the nineteenth century - the disgrace of a divorce. Bertha's ex mother-in-law was so upset that her son had become divorced, for reasons not known to this day, she made sure that nobody from her side of her family would ever have anything to do with her ex daughter-in-law or her one granddaughter from that marriage. An older single mother was a rare person as opposed to unfortunate or unlucky younger girls known to every generation. After the divorce Bertha maintained herself by taking in lodgers and working at industrial fairs selling souvenir badges which she made at home. A few years later Bertha married a divorced cigar maker. Bertha's daughter Hanna had a great fondness for her step-father Jerphaas, who was not Jewish.

Bertha's mother and Erich's father were related as they had a common great grandfather, a descendant of the possible pedlar mentioned earlier. As can be imagined it was a very large family by now with many cousins but this part of family had kept in contact over the years. Bertha was aware of the increasing plight of the Jews in Germany. She belonged to an underground network which helped those Jews who had left Germany and also involved her daughter Hanna. On one occasion Hanna helped to smuggle a woman from Belgium to Holland by walking along the sandy coastal beaches with her where there were no border posts. If they had been intercepted the woman was to act as if she was deaf and dumb but fortunately they were not challenged. At that time Hanna was engaged to an older man who was a ship's purser on board a merchant vessel. On one occasion one of Hanna's friends asked her to accompany her on visit to a fortune teller, which she reluctantly did. As they entered the fortune teller's room they stopped and stood near the door. The fortune teller said 'You will not marry the man you are engaged to.' Hanna looked at her friend and was surprised to hear that the remark was addressed not to her friend but to her. She naturally disregarded this remark.

The two brothers who had illegally arrived in the Netherlands came to Amsterdam and lodged in Bertha's flat. They had entry visas for a number of South American countries but were unable to board the sailings in the Netherlands. They decided to go to London where one of Hanna's married cousins lived to find the earliest suitable sailing to their chosen destination. Plans were made for Hans' wife Wally and their son Gunter, who had just turned three, to move to Holland. In the meantime Hanna had fallen in love with Erich and accompanied the two brothers to England in the summer of 1939. The loving couple were married that August at the local Registry Office with Bertha coming to London for the wedding. They started their married life living in two rooms on the ground floor of a mid Victorian house and sharing the bathroom facilities with their neighbours in the basement.

After the Registry Office ceremony -
Zus, Myra, Hanna, Erich and Bertha

# LETTERS

SO WE NOW HAVE SOME OF THE BACKGROUND TO the correspondence that survives after all this time. The first 'letter' is in fact a postcard written on 29th August 1939 by Bertha aboard the boat returning to the Netherlands after the wedding.

---

*Dear Hanna. Erich and Hans*

*I am writing this postcard to you from the boat. There were no problems getting my luggage onto the boat. It will be an hour before we arrive at Vlissingen and I have been lucky as I have not been seasick up to now and do not expect to be so before we arrive. The weather is rather pleasant and my face is a little sunburnt as I forgot to bring the Nivea cream with me. Hanna how is your throat? Gargle a lot and if it does not get better do not go to visit Myra*[1] *but stay in bed. If you cannot go Erich will take care of it. Did Erich you and Hans go off to the woods again today to pick blackberries? Hanna I think that I left the old round flat bottle, you know the one, the one that*

1 Myra - Hanna's married cousin living in London.

*you gave me. If you find it can you give it to your cousin Zus[2] to take back. I will finish for now as the boat has almost arrived and land is in sight. I have just read in the trade magazine that the farmers are already spreading their manure and that there are delays in the postal service so please keep this in mind. All best wishes and kisses for you from your Moeke.[3]*
*I forgot Hans, but he is also included.*

*B Jordaan[4]*
*Zuideramstelaan 213*
*South Amsterdam*

---

A few days later at 11am on 3rd September 1939 England declared war on Germany as Poland had been invaded by Germany. By the little Treaty of Versailles England, with others, was a guarantor of Polish independence.

In the Spring of 1940 Hanna went back to Amsterdam to see her mother. It seems that all the boat tickets to return to England had been sold out. So at far greater expense she tried to get a seat on an aircraft back to England which was at war with Germany. No air tickets were available from Amsterdam so she took the train to Brussels and there managed to get an aeroplane ticket back to England. From October 1939 air flights from neutral countries such as Belgium, Holland and Denmark were only allowed to use coastal airports such as Shoreham, a very small airport near Brighton. The kind of planes that were in service then seated twelve people and were propeller driven models. From the next letter we learn that Hanna had found work as a typist for the Dutch Government in exile.

2 Zus - a sister of Kinny and Lex, who all her life liked any excuse to travel somewhere.
3 Moeke - common Dutch term of endearment for mother - "mummy".
4 Jordaan - Bertha having taken the name of her second husband.

*Amsterdam* *21/4/40*

*Dear Hanna and Erich*

*It is Sunday again and I wanted to answer your letter which I received on Thursday afternoon and is lying right next to me. The post is much faster if you use Air Mail and it is worth paying the extra postage, as I did at the start when you left home, rather than having to wait for the post to arrive and worrying. Hanna asks if I receive my post quickly. I have not received that letter yet and do not expect to receive it. I now know what I can send and the list*[5] *is not too long. If you have the same nice weather we are enjoying here today you would certainly have gone to the park. You should be sensible enough to take advantage of the fact that that Erich is now earning a little bit of money as there is little chance that you will be able to save for the foreseeable future. If it were me I would spend a little on myself. You know how far you got when you tried saving. As Tante Rosine*[6] *has not yet moved I will send your letter on to her in Eindhoven tomorrow. It will be Monday when Tini and Lini are coming to visit me. (Tini is staying with Lini for the time being until she decides if she is going to rent a flat here in Amsterdam.) Tini has to go to R for a fitting and she is a good customer of theirs. Lotte has not heard from America for a long time. Tomorrow, after I have done the laundry and if I am not too tired, as it is the laundry for at least four people for four weeks, I will go to Tante Regina*[7] *as usual, otherwise I will go on Tuesday, to discuss the linen and how to send it. I will arrange to send as many clothes as possible that you left behind when you went to England. Tomorrow I will send you by parcel post the nut mixture you wrote about in your last letter and will also include a pound of coffee syrup (which you should keep in a sealed tin) with some other things that you have forgotten. I will write and let you know what I am adding to your linen when I send*

5 List - a list of goods that were permitted to be sent to England.

6 Rosine (Tante) - sister-in-law of Bertha and mother of Tini, Eefke, Lini and Ben.

7 Regina (Tante) - wife of Bertha's brother Isaac.

*it to you. Don't you think that this business with Norway is terrible and it is good that England quickly came to their aid? Hanna, you ask how I am getting on here as where you are you may hear that things are much worse than they are. I cannot write anything about that. You read your newspapers and they will report how things are. I think that I would like to go and visit Eefke soon but do not know if it will be possible. When sending the parcel I will make sure to wrap up Erich's typewriter well as it is old and has to arrive safely as otherwise it will be of no use to anyone. Hanna why did you write to me to ask me to deduct the cost of the coffee syrup when you know full well that I will not do that? What I wrote to you about Adele has already completely finished and it only gave her short term joy. It is a pity as she deserves a good man and would dearly like to find one. Hanna you wrote that you had already used the dried soup vegetables. If I can buy some here I will dry them and send them to you. Were you able to buy a lighter for me for Hans' birthday? You have not mentioned anything about that. Perhaps this week or next week I am going to Ernst and will find out what he intends to do with that money. I have heard no more from Sternfeld and there is no change in the situation of the Loewenstein family. What is the position with Wally[8], will you be able to do anything for her? She is on tenterhooks to find out. Before I forget I want to wish you a good Yomtov[9] and hope that your wishes are fulfilled, and also for Hans, and that we may soon have a good lasting peace and that all people can live their lives in peace and quiet. As long as the head of AH[10] has not been smashed in there can be no peace. If the prayers of many people are heard it will happen very soon. Hanna on Wednesday evening Ro Ruedelsheim was here asking after you and looked at me in a strange way after hearing the whole story. I told her that you had written to her and that you would write a lengthier letter to her shortly which she is now waiting for. I enjoyed her being here for a while that evening and that she at least asked after you. During*

8 Wally - Hans's wife who was living in the Netherlands at that time with their son Gunter.

9 Yomtov - a Jewish greeting used on festivals meaning have a good day. The Passover festival usually falls in March/April.

10 AH - Adolf Hitler.

*the week I bought some fine wool so that I could start knitting a cardigan for you. It is beige and will be very pretty as you will see when it is finished. This afternoon after I have returned from my walk I will make the spice mixture for the letters[11] for Erich and Hans. I will bake them but I will not make letters out of them as it is too much work but instead I will prepare filled speculaas[12] biscuits and think that they, and you, will find them very tasty. I will send it in the parcel with the nut mixture and you can write to me and let me know how it tasted. I have not yet sent the blue skirt to Grete[13]. I do not know if Oome will get time off work to congratulate Oma. You will hear about that in the next letter. I also wanted to write to you that with your last letter we received a small printed yellow piece of paper which said in English to make the letters short and legible (especially legible). I think it is better that you know this so that you can conform. Hanna you write that you go to the street market with Erich on a Tuesday afternoon but street markets are not your scene. It has more to do with being with Erich than going to the market. Hanna have you written to Oom Issy[14] yet, it is something that you still have to do. I think that I have written about everything and I will be waiting all week again to get your letter filled with good news. Perhaps I will go to see Julia again this week. I have to write something about Gunter. He cannot keep a secret. Last week he said to me "Auntie, who was that woman who came into grandma's room?" Yesterday he went to the beach with her and when he came back he told me that Julia had fallen asleep there, amongst other things. Last week I bought him a bucket and spade which he took with him to the beach. But now I must really finish because Wally and Julie have come to collect me to go for a walk in the park as it would be a shame not to enjoy such wonderful weather. Please send my regards to Myra, Lege, Hans, and the Sandersen and Hern families. Best wishes for Erich, a kiss for you, Hanna, from your*

11 Letters - it is a Dutch custom to make or buy confectionary or chocolate in the form of the initial letter of a person's name for their birthday, Christmas or other special occasion.

12 Speculaas - a popular Dutch spiced biscuit, often in the shape of a windmill.

13 Grete - the sister of Hans and Erich.

14 Oom Issy - one of Bertha's brothers.

*loving mother. I am pleased that Erich is comfortable with you going to work. We have just come back from the park where we took some snaps of Gunter which Hans would dearly like to have and will send them with my next letter. Bye*

---

### May 1940

10 Dawn Friday 3.55am - Germany invades the Netherlands without any declaration of war.
13 Queen Wilhelmina, the Dutch queen, flees to England.
14 Rotterdam is flattened by bombing causing over 30,000 casualties including almost 1,000 deaths and over 80,000 people become homeless.
15 German troops occupy Amsterdam and to avoid further civilian slaughter the government decides to capitulate. The Netherlands is now under German occupation.
16 Press censorship imposed.
19 Amsterdam time now changed to Berlin Time (Central European Time).
21 The Dutch radio station AVRO dismisses all Jewish employees.
22 Dutch Premier De Geer begins working with the Nazis.
24 Dutch Queen speaks to Dutch nation via BBC radio in London.
24 Dutch army ordered to demobilise.
29 Arthur Seyss-Inquart installed as supreme Parliamentary Governor of the Netherlands.

### June 1940

1 Tea and coffee now rationed.
5 Petrol now rationed.
15 Bread and flour now rationed.
19 Seizure of all Dutch horses, ships, cars and buses or-

dered by Goering.
21 Dutch States General/Council of State disbanded by Germans.
22 SS rounds up 31 Jews in the town of Roermond.

JULY 1940

2 Jews prohibited from serving as air raid wardens.
3 Use of names associated with Dutch Royal family now forbidden.
4 Anti Nazi speeches forbidden.
4 Listening to non-German foreign radio broadcasts forbidden.
19 Showing of Anti-Nazi films banned.
19 Nazis imprison 231 prominent citizens in Buchenwald Concentration Camp.
21 Dutch Communist Party outlawed.
22 Prime Minister de Geer meets Hitler for peace talks.
24 First illegal publication 'Pieter 't Hoen' appears.
28 Radio Orange, based in London, starts broadcasting to the Netherlands.
31 Being homosexual is forbidden.

AUGUST 1940

3 Cinemas banned from showing French or English films.
3 Under the guise of animal welfare provisions Jewish ritual slaughter is banned.
5 Synagogue in the coastal resort of Zandvoort is blown up.
6 Jews could no longer be recruited into the Dutch civil service and those Jews who were employed could not be promoted.
12 Textiles products are now rationed.
20 Dutch civil servants could now be dismissed without cause.
20 Jews of German origin ordered to leave the Hague

Biedermann

E.F (G) 2/39.

Dutch.

ENQUIRY FORM

DATE 14-5-40

NAME: KANN Mrs Hannah

ADDRESS: 28 Hemstal Rd NW6

TELEPHONE:

ENQUIRING FOR: Bic Jordaan Biedermann

NATIONALITY Dutch

ADDRESS Minerva Amstellaan 213 Amsterdam Z. Holland

De Jongh Biedermann

Can have her mother to live –

-7 AOUT 1940

Antwoord op keerzijde

14-5-40

The above may be an historic document as it has to be one of the very first Dutch Red Cross enquiry forms - dated 14 May 1940, four days after the German invasion of the Netherlands. The form's makeshift nature makes this evident. Although dated 14th May 1940 it was only processed in Geneva by the Swiss Red Cross on 7th August 1940. The reply was checked in England on 25th October 1940.

Plaats voor antwoord
(hoogstens 25 woorden, uitsluitend voor persoonlijke- of familie- aangelegenheden).

Wij allen ook Omas maken het best. Ben zeer ongerust om jullie. Laat ons of Ernst spoedig iets van jullie hooren, indien mogelijk telegrafisch
Moeke.

COMITE INTERNATIONAL DE LA CROIX-ROUGE GENEVE

25 OCT 1940

The translation of the reply in Dutch above, limited to 25 words, reads: "We, including Omas, are all managing well. Am most concerned about you. Let us, or Ernst, quickly hear news from you, even by telegram if this is possible. Moeke"

**Het Nederlandsche Roode Kruis**

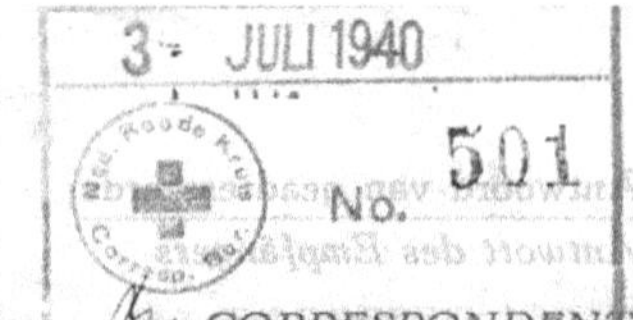

3 - JULI 1940

No. 501

Formulier, na invulling, in te zenden aan het *CORRESPONDENTIE-BUREAU* van het Nederlandsche Roode Kruis, Carel van Bylandtlaan 10, Den Haag.

VERZOEK
door tusschenkomst van het Duitsche Roode Kruis aan het Internationale Comité van het Roode Kruis te Genève om inlichtingen.

*ANTRAG*
*durch das Deutsche Rote Kreuz an das Internationale Komitee vom Roten Kreuz in Genf auf Nachrichtenvermittlung*

1. Afzender / *Absender* B. Jordaan-Biedermann
(naam, voornaam en adres)
*(Name, Taufname und Adresse)*
Zuider Amstellaan 16 II, Amsterdam Zuid.

Verzoekt aan
*Bittet an*

2. Geadresseerde / *Empfänger* Familie Kann-Crost, 28, Hemstal road,
(naam, voornaam en adres)
*(Name, Taufname und Adresse)*
London NW 6.

het volgende mede te deelen:
*folgendes zu übermitteln:*
(ten hoogste 25 woorden uitsluitend persoonlijke en familieaangelegenheden betreffende)
*(Höchstzahl 25 Worte nur persönliche und Familieangelegenheiten betreffend)*

Lieve kinderen,
Moeke, Oom, Wally, Gunter, Oma zijn allen gezond. Zouden gaarne langs dezen weg van jullie iets vernemen. Allen feliciteeren hartelijk voor Hanna's verjaardag.

21 AOUT 1940

Handteekening
*Unterschrift*

3. Geadresseerde antwoordt aan ommezijde
*Empfänger antwortet umseitig*

B. Jordaan-Biedermann

This Red Cross enquiry form was sent by Hanna's mother dated 3 July 1940. The message reads "Dear Children Moeke, Oom, Wally, Gunter, Oma are all well. Would like to hear from you using this method of communicating. All send happy returns for Hanna's birthday".

4. Antwoord van geadresseerde
*Antwort des Empfängers*

(ten hoogste 25 woorden uitsluitend persoonlijke en familieaangelegenheden betreffende)

*(Höchstzahl 25 Worte nur persönliche und Familieangelegenheiten betreffend)*

*Handteekening*
*Unterschrift*

By now Dutch Red Cross had been taken over and is being operated by the German Red Cross.

and costal areas and to register with the Aliens Department.

23 Queen dismisses Prime Minister de Geer.

30 A Jew is defined as anyone with only one Jewish grandparent - a stricter definition than in the German Nuremberg race laws.

31 Soap is now rationed.

## September 1940

3 Gerbrandy forms Dutch government in exile in London.

4 Gerbrandy becomes Prime Minister of Dutch government in exile.

11 Nazi collaborator Anton Mussert, leader of Dutch NSB Nazis, establishes Dutch SS.

14 Meat now rationed.

14 Jews banned from attending or trading in Amsterdam markets.

19 Gentile women forbidden to work in Jewish homes

23 Mussert's first meeting with Hitler.

26 All Jewish publications banned except for the Nazi controlled 'Jewish Weekly'.

30 Civil Service not to employ any more Jews or promote those that are employed.

## October 1940

1 Identity Cards introduced for everyone aged 15 or over.

5 Civil servants had to sign a form attesting that they were Aryans - Form A - or Non Aryans - Form B. The forms had to be signed within a week.

17 Special Identity cards introduced for Jews.

20 Cheese now rationed.

21 First RAF drop anti-Nazi leaflets on the Netherlands.

22 All businesses with either one Jewish owner or one Jewish director had to register with the German authorities or face a sizeable fine.

24 Protestant churches protest against the dismissal of Jewish civil servants.
30 Every government official had to sign an affidavit that neither he, his wife, fiance, parents or grandparents were Jewish.

Hanna had visited her mother in Amsterdam in April 1940 and returned from Belgium to her husband in London just before the German invasion of the Netherlands on 10th May 1940. (It can not have helped that she had renewed her acquaintance with Erich's family in Duisburg in July 1939. The visit would have been shown in her passport.) The powers in England decided that she, in common with the passport holders of other previously neutral countries, should be interned. In Hanna's case this was on the Isle of Man. No reason was ever given to those neutrals interned other that there was a war on. Many of the Jewish refugees from Germany and Austria were sent to the Isle of Man, and others even overseas. They could not, supposedly, make contact with anyone or do any damage had there been a fifth columnist (subversive agent) amongst them. (In fact on the Isle of Man the internees set up lectures, concerts and other cultural activities while literally behind barbed wire.) Hanna was married to an enemy alien and had returned a matter of weeks before the German invasion of the Netherlands. This could have been seen as an ideal way to plant a spy on British soil. Bertha complains that she had not received a letter since 13 June which suggests that Hanna might have been interned shortly afterwards or during the summer of 1940. After appearing before a local Isle of Man tribunal in October it must have been decided that she was not a threat to national security. Heavily pregnant Hanna was released about ten days after the hearing. Ronald was subsequently born in London on 28 October 1940.

### November 1940

1 Introduction of a 'curfew' in the Netherlands from noon to 4pm.

4 Eggs and cake are now rationed.
15 Natural gas and electricity are now rationed.
21 No more new schools to be built in the Netherlands.
21 All Jewish civil servants are dismissed.
22 In Delft 500 students protest against the Nazis.
23 Jewish university staff and Jewish Court officials are dismissed.
26 Students in Leiden protest against the Nazis.
28 Dutch law professor Rudolph Cleveringa arrested by Nazis for protesting at the dismissal of Jewish colleagues.

---

*Dear Hanna Erich and Hans* *10/11/40*

*Hopefully you are all very well as we are, including Ida and Therese*[15]*. The last news I received was your letter of 13/6 which I answered immediately and since then I have heard nothing more, nor from Ernst. I am writing this letter in the hope that you will receive it in the best of health. As I heard from your cousin Myra you are expecting a baby which I look forward to with great pleasure, but only when I have heard, with God's help, of the safe delivery. I hope and pray Hanna that when the time comes the good Lord will give you the help that you will then need. You can understand how sorry I am that I cannot be with you at that time but with God's help everything will run it's normal course. In the meantime I have knitted some cute baby things that you could take with you when you come to visit me or I could bring them to you. I am here in Eindhoven with Tante Rosine who is in hospital having had her appendix taken out. She is going home next Saturday. I am to look after her household in the meantime and will stay here with her until the St Nicholas celebration (5th December). Many happy returns for your birthday Erich and by that time you may be a father. I wish you all, especially Hans, all the best. Love and kisses from you loving mother. Also best regards*

15 Therese - one of Bertha's sisters.

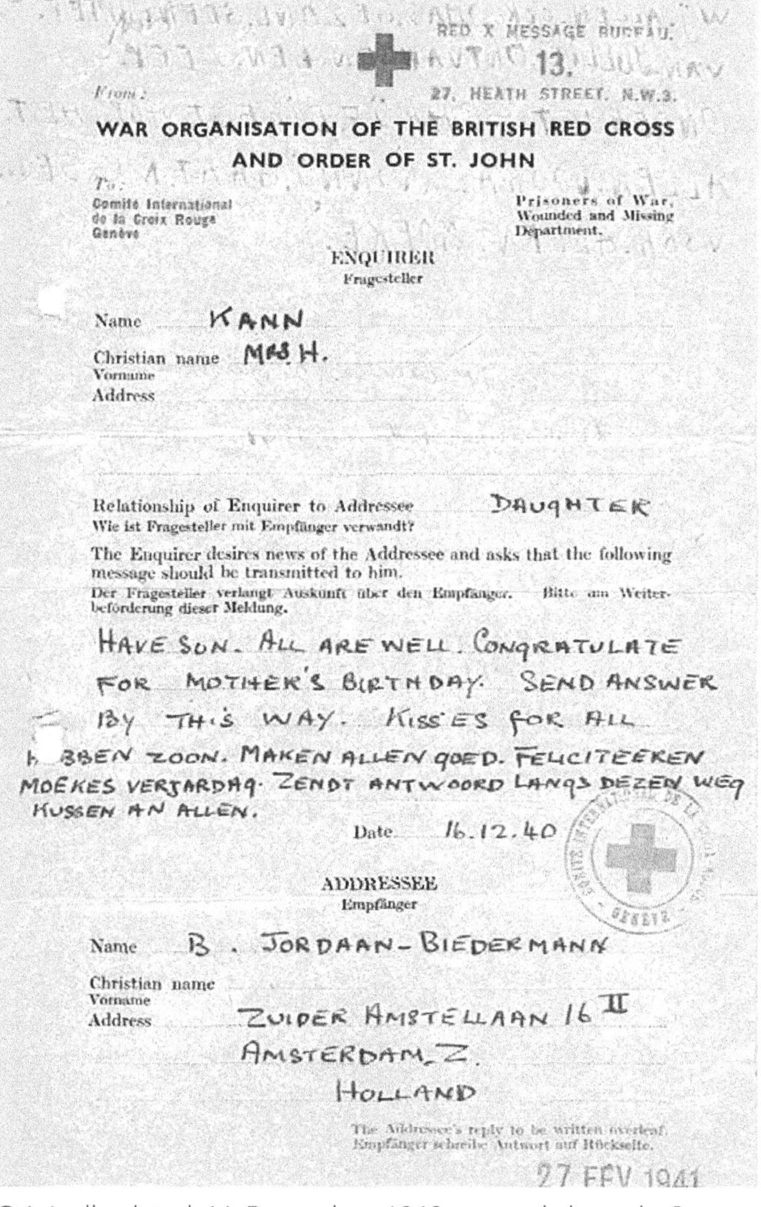

RED X MESSAGE BUREAU.
13.
27, HEATH STREET, N.W.3.

From:

WAR ORGANISATION OF THE BRITISH RED CROSS
AND ORDER OF ST. JOHN

To:
Comité International
de la Croix Rouge
Genève

Prisoners of War,
Wounded and Missing
Department.

ENQUIRER
Fragesteller

Name KANN
Christian name MRS. H.
Vorname
Address

Relationship of Enquirer to Addressee DAUGHTER
Wie ist Fragesteller mit Empfänger verwandt?

The Enquirer desires news of the Addressee and asks that the following message should be transmitted to him.
Der Fragesteller verlangt Auskunft über den Empfänger. Bitte um Weiterbeförderung dieser Meldung.

HAVE SON. ALL ARE WELL. CONGRATULATE FOR MOTHER'S BIRTHDAY. SEND ANSWER BY THIS WAY. KISSES FOR ALL

HEBBEN ZOON. MAKEN ALLEN GOED. FELICITEEREN MOEKES VERJARDAG. ZENDT ANTWOORD LANGS DEZEN WEG KUSSEN AN ALLEN.

Date 16.12.40

ADDRESSEE
Empfänger

Name B. JORDAAN-BIEDERMANN
Christian name
Vorname
Address ZUIDER AMSTELLAAN 16 II
AMSTERDAM Z.
HOLLAND

The Addressee's reply to be written overleaf.
Empfänger schreibe Antwort auf Rückseite.

27 FEV 1941

Originally dated 16 December 1940, passed through Geneva on 27 February 1941. The reply is dated 21 March 1941. This passed through Geneva again on 21 April 1941 before it was examined by the English authorities. The Dutch shown below is a translation of the English.

WIJ.ALLEN.OOK.OMAS.GEZOND.GEEN.BRIEF.
VAN.JULLIE.ONTVANGEN.BEN.ZEER.
ONGERUST.SCHRIJF.DIREGT.HOE.HET.
ALLEN.VOORAL.RONNIJ.GAAT.KUSSEN.
VOOR.ALLEN. MOEKE.

B. Jordaan. Biedermann
Amsterdam 21 Maart 1941.

PASSED
P.123

21 AVR 1941

The reply in Dutch reads: "We are all well including Oma. Have not received a letter from you. Am most worried. Write by return how you are, especially, Ronny. kisses for all. Moeke" *from grandma Ida, Therese, Tante Rosine, Wally and Gunter. Please let me know as quickly as possible when the baby arrives. Ida is also waiting for news and I wrote her a very nice letter this week which is something I am sure that she will enjoyed reading.*

*We have moved and my new address is Zuideramstellaan 16 II.*

---

*4*[16] *29/12/40*

*Dear Hanna, Erich, Hans and little Ronald*

*Firstly I have to ask how you all are and hope that you are well as we all are. Why is it that I do not get replies to any of my letters? This is the fourth time of writing and as you can imagine I would like to hear something from you. How is the not so new mother and is the little baby putting on weight? How are his happy daddy and his uncle Hans? Do you ever see Jo's*[17] *brother? Jo and Lini regularly receive post from him. Yesterday I heard from Adele that you received a letter from Ida, very nice. Because I do not know if you received my earlier letters I will have to repeat what I wrote earlier again. I spent 9 weeks with Tante Rosine to help run her home while she spent four weeks in hospital troubled by her appendix, and she has also had an operation on her foot. I got home just a week ago. As you will have heard from Ernst Wally and Gunter are no longer with me. If you write to Ernst ask him if he could let me also read your letter. Hanna and Erich I have made such lovely outfits and I can see him wearing these woollies in my mind's eye. Last week, just before Christmas, I received a parcel from Ida with four saucepan holders. I have sent her some very nice flowers on several occasions as I know that she is very fond of these and that it is the best thing*

16 The number 4 is shown at the top of the letter. Possibly earlier letters had also been numbered.
17 Jo - married to Lini, one of Hanna's cousins. Jo's brother had worked in London since 1917.

*to send her. Hanna are you feeding the child yourself? Please write more fully about the little treasure and if it is possible please send a photo of you both and of him. Erich, I once again send you many happy returns for you on your birthday as I have done on three previous occasions. I had a telegram from Myra to announce the birth of the baby but since then I have heard no more. Do you still live in the same neighbourhood where Mr Sanders lives or nearer to where Myra now lives? I am going to finish now but will write again in fortnight but in the meantime I do hope that I will have heard something from you. With the New Year approaching I wish you all goodness and good luck.*
*Greetings and kisses for you all from your loving mother, Grandpa and aunties.*
*Hanna and Erich look after little Ronald well and make sure that nothing harms him. Write to me quickly as I am hungry for news of all and everything as I have not heard anything from you for such a long time. Again kisses from your mother.*
*Oome also sends greetings. Also Julie, Lotte and Mrs Rosenzwieg and especially not forgetting Tante Rosine. All our friends, too numerous to mention, also send their best wishes. Goodbye and all the best.*

*Sender: B Jordaan Zuideramstellaan 16 II - mother of the addressee.*

---

## January 1941

1 Start date of having to buy an annual permit to listen to the radio.

9 Jews prohibited from entering theatres and cinemas.

10 All Jews or any person with one Jewish grandparent residing in the Netherlands must register with the authorities. Failure to do so is punishable by five years in prison or confiscation of property, or both. A Jew is defined as having at least one Jewish grandparent.

16 Jews living in Amsterdam had to declare, amongst other things, the location of Jewish owned shops and

houses, places of worship, schools, cultural institutions and the tram and bus services which they used.
31 Anti-German demonstration takes place in Haarlem.

The next letter is not dated but it refers to the letter from Hanna at the end of November and it is possible that this was not received until the early months of 1941.

---

*Dear little Ronny, Hanna, Erich and Hans*

*I cannot say how elated I was to receive your letter of 29/11 and I was in such a happy state that you can well imagine. From that I understand you are all doing well and that naturally gives me great pleasure. It is exceptional that everything went so well with the birth of little Ronny and we should thank the good Lord for that. I enjoyed your brief description of little Ronny, what he looks like and that he resembled Erich. He must be a handsome little lad. Erich this compliment is aimed at you, and Hanna, do you like your husband receiving compliments? Have you got all that you need for the little one? Does he get enough nourishment? From what you write it seems that Hanna is feeding him herself which is the best for him. Erich make sure that she eats properly so that the child gets good quality milk so that he can grow. Now I will tell you what I have knitted for my little darling. Three pretty all in one suits, you know the ones I mean Hanna, each with matching little bootees, a little shirt and a very smart little jacket; a couple of nice bibs; and now I am busy with a very smart little romper set. Everything I mention is knitted in a fine ply soft wool. When I have finished the little set that I am currently working on I will start on something else. I have made everything on the large side so that he can wear it for a long time. I still have a supply of white wool suitable for babies. Please write and let me know what you would like me to knit for you as it is the same to me whatever I knit. Have you got a good supply of nappies and make sure that the child does not lie in the wet too long as otherwise he will get a rash, and make sure you use lots of cotton wool and often apply talcum powder which will help prevent him getting a nappy rash. Hans must seem like a giant when he holds the tiny baby in his hands. I visited everyone to whom you sent birthday wishes in your letter. They all send their congratulations to you on the birth of Ronny and send their best wishes to Hans. Of late I am spending a lot of time with the Rozenzweigs and go there as I do not have a lot to do in the afternoon other than sew. I help them and they help me by to bring my wardrobe up to scratch. I will leave a small space for them as they want to add a few words. Yesterday I was at Ro's who congratulates you and sends you her best wishes. She will also add a few words to my next letter. Tante Rosine and her children congratulate you and send their best wishes as do all your other aunts and uncles. Eefke and her family are well as is the family of Kinny.*[18] *Hanna have you already got a pram? Did Ronny get something nice in his little shoe*[19] *for St Nicholas? Please buy him something nice from me for St Nicholas. Erich you will surely have enjoyed celebrating your birthday with your son in your lap who was able to arrive before Christmas. Hans, soon the time will come when you will have your wife in your arms and your son on your lap, perhaps in time for your birthday. In any case I hope that all of you will help Hans celebrate his birthday, which I think is in March. I will finish now as I have to leave room for some others. I have already written to Oma Ida and Auntie Therese and have told the whole family. Please write quickly to let me know how you all are and specially how little Ronny is getting on. Perhaps his daddy has taken a photo of the little darling and could send it to me. I wish you all the very best, excellent health and give you all a great big kiss, from your loving Moeke. Grandpa and Auntie would like to send their own kisses for my little darling. I am very pleased that Erich is*

18 Kinny - married to Bertha's nephew Sem.

19 Little shoe - rather than hanging up a stocking on Christmas Eve the Dutch custom allows young children to leave one of their shoes near the fireplace before going to bed. If they are lucky Sint Nicholas may have visited their home during the night and left a small present to be found in the morning. This happens in the days leading up to the arrival of Sint Nicholas and Black Pieter from Spain on 5th December, the Eve of the Saint's Day. The festival is celebrated more than Christmas Day itself.

*working so that things are getting better. It is nice that Lilo goes with you to see Ronny, her parents are well and send you and her regards. Cheerio and hope that you all will be here with me soon.*

[Underneath and in the margins are greetings from various people.]

---

*Dear Hanna, Erich Hans and my little darling* *9/2/41*

*Hopefully you are all well and that things are as you would like them to be, especially for my little Ronny. I can let you know that over here we are all well. In the meantime you will surely have received my letters in which I wrote the fullest details about my birthday. Hanna and Erich write to me in your very next letter everything about Ronny as I am very curious to know everything about him. Hanna if you are very busy just leave things and look after the child which is more important than your work. I told my niece Ida all about Ronny and said to her that she could add her own short note to go with my letter to you so as to save her the postage which she did. She was pleased to do so and I am sending it with this letter. Last week I sent her a nice bunch of flowers, which is all that she seems to be interested in these days, and she came round this very morning specially to thank me. It is a shame that the weather is so bad because the flowers have become scarce and expensive. As long as I can afford it I will send her flowers every three or four weeks. She is always very pleased when she receives the flowers. Hanna if you speak to Myra please send her my regards. I am going to see her mother this afternoon to wish her a happy birthday which, as you know, is on 10 February and will also do it in you name. How are the gentlemen and will you able to make some jam again this year? Erich you wrote that you now know what it is be a father. But does your son allow his father a good night's sleep or does he cry every now and then during the night? I think not, as with such a capable father he can only be a good son. Erich make sure that Hanna eats properly and does not go on a diet as the child will not get enough food. And Hans how are you? You never let us hear about yourself. Wally wrote to me yesterday that she is quite pleased where she is. The note from Ida is from last week and as she was here this morning she asked me again to send you her regards. I have finished knitting the little trousers I have been making for Ronny and am using the same wool to knit a little jacket to match so that the little man will have a suit. So my dears the page is full. Write to us as we are always curious about how you are getting on and especially about little Ronny. Hanna take special care of him. You asked if we were working, unfortunately we are still not working. All friends and family without exception send their greetings. We send our heartfelt good wishes and kisses from your loving mother and Oma. Naturally greetings for Hans are included and a separate special kiss for my little Ronny.*

[Written upside down at the top of the letter]

*I hope that you can send me a small photograph of the child next time you write.*
*Tante Bertha Biedermann wrote four letters to her son in law in Lisbon and has not had any reply. I am enclosing a pre-paid envelope for your reply, please do the same.*

[and down the left hand side of the body of the letter]

*Eefke*[20] *spent a few days with her little daughter Rozenike. I have just received a letter from Myra and they are well. Bye.*

---

FEBRUARY 1941

1 Several physicians arrested in Hilversum.
5 All doctors have to be registered.
9 Nazi collaborators destroy Cafe Alcazar in Amsterdam's Jewish district as the cafe refused to display

20 Eefke - Bertha's niece, a sibling of Tini, Lini and Ben.

the sign 'Jews Not Permitted'. A riot ensues and a Nazi is killed.

10 First edition of the underground Anti-Nazi newspaper 'Het Parool' appears edited by the same person who was behind the illegal publication 'Pieter 't Hoen' the previous July.

11 Restrictive measures passed against Jewish students.

11 German security service in the Netherlands complains about Dutch anti-German sentiment.

11 Pitched battle between the WA, the paramilitary arm of the Dutch Fascist German sympathisers, and young Jews in Waterlooplein, Amsterdam.

12 Jews ordered to hand in all their weapons.

12 Old established Jewish neighbourhood in Amsterdam encircled with barbed wire.

13 The Jewish Council was established under Nazi instruction consisting of 20 members, including rabbis, lawyers and middle class business men. All Dutch people had to carry an Identity Card to obtain their ration cards. Jewish people had theirs stamped with a 'J'. This way the Nazis knew that there were 159,806 full Jews, 19,561 half-Jews (from a mixed marriage), and about 5,000 quarter Jews (one Jewish grandparent).

13 Nazi leaders attack Jewish Council.

14 Jews no longer allowed to own any company or commercial undertaking.

17 Amsterdam shipyard workers go on strike to prevent Dutchmen being sent to Germany for forced labour.

19 Nazi police storm the Koco Ice Cream parlour in Amsterdam and are driven off by young Jews.

22 425 people arrested as Himmler orders the first round up of Jews in Amsterdam who are deported to Buchenwald and Mauthausen concentration camps. Only two survived the incarceration.

24 Trial of 43 members of the Geuzen resistance group

opens in the Hague.

25 Call for a General Strike is made in Amsterdam protesting at the persecution of the Jews. The strike continues, with support in many Dutch towns, but was violently suppressed by the Germans.

27 General Strike ended by German use of force.

28 Germans now require any unemployed Dutchman to perform compulsory labour.

28 Restrictive measures applied to Jewish charities.

### March 1941

1 Dutch Labour Service opens its first Labour Camp.

4 15 Resistance fighters in the Geuzen group and three Communist strike leaders are sentenced to death in the Hague.

12 Dutch radio studios AVRO confiscated by Germans.

12 Small Jewish business are liquidated but Germans begin to 'Aryanise' larger Jewish businesses sending in supervisors. Jewish property previously registered is taken over.

12 Jewish owned companies are now forbidden.

13 15 of the Geuzen resistance and three communists are executed.

20 Evacuation of all the residents of Jewish work village Nieuwe Schans. Set up in 1934 for refugee Jews from Germany and Austria to prepare for a life in Palestine . All who were arrested sent to Mauthausen concentration camp.

26 Leading Nazi Rost van Tonningen put in charge of the Dutch National Bank.

31 Office for Jewish Emigration is established.

The following letter is not dated but from the contents it would seem to be appropriate to be included at this point.

*Dear Hanna, Erich, Hans and darling Ronny*

*Although I have not had a reply to the last letter I sent you (which of course is not possible) I am writing to you again in the hope that this finds you all in the best of health. First of all how is my darling little Ronny, and is he getting bigger? Hanna are you able to cope and care for him? I expect that the hospital will have told you what to do. Are you able to feed him properly? Make sure that you eat enough as otherwise the child will not get sufficient nourishment. Erich do you take the baby out for walks or are you waiting for summer and better weather? Have you already got a pram for him? Hanna you asked me to write with more detailed information about Wally and Gunter. Since the end of May they have lived in Oostlaan where Else and Max lived. Since they left I have been able to let a room. They both often visited us and occasionally slept here. I have been out with Wally and frequently visited them at their home. I visit them by bicycle. Of late I have taken to riding a bicycle again, it saves a lot of money on tram fares, and that is why I bought an old bike. Since Christmas she has moved again. She is now in a big boarding house with several of her other friends near Assen.*[21] *Else, Max and Leonard are also very happy there. She has written to me several times. I forwarded the last letter I received from you to her. Did she drop you a line? She wrote to congratulate me on my birthday and now, because they were not with me on my birthday, have sent them a little parcel with various delicacies we had at my birthday tea, which incidentally I sent off this afternoon. In the next letter that I write she will add a few words which I expect will be within the next 8-10 days. Hanna and Erich will you also write to us every eight days or every fortnight then we will not have to wait so long for post from you. Naturally I am very keen to hear your good news but I specially want to know as much as possible about Ronny and if it is possible perhaps you can send me a photo of Ronny. Hanna I dreamt this week that you said to me 'Moeke, buy some flowers for your birthday on behalf of Ronny'. So I went to the florist and bought a mixed bunch of long lasting flowers which were*

21 Assen - the capital town of the northern Dutch province of Drente.

*to be delivered and attached a little card with best wishes from little Ronny for my birthday. They proudly stood on the birthday table and next to it a vase of red tulips from Hanna and Erich. I had a very nice birthday, but in the morning I cried because you, the main people in my life, were not there. Eefke and little Rosine[22] visited Tante Rosine last week. Eefke's husband had previously visited on many occasions. Kinny is doing splendidly and thanks you for your congratulations. And all the others whom you congratulated for their birthdays thank you and wish you all the best. All your relations without fail are very supportive of you and the Rozenzwieg family also send their best wishes. All these greetings and good wishes naturally include Hans.*

*Well I suppose I had better finish now as the page is full. As always I wish you the very best and heartfelt best wishes and kisses from your ever loving mother granny and auntie. Separately a lot of kisses for Ronny also from his other granny and best wishes for you two from her as well. Rosa Cracou also sends you congratulations on the birth of Ronny.*

---

*Dear Hanna, Erich, Hans and my little Ronny* *5/3/41*

*I hope that you have received the letters that I recently wrote to you (of which there were three) and which to date I have not yet received a single reply and hope that you are well and in the best of health when you received them. Every day I expect to receive a letter from you in which I hope only to receive good news from you and especially a lot of news about my little darling. By now I expect that he is already smiling and is allowed to drink a little fruit juice. Hanna please be very careful as the little ones are likely to get intestinal problems so do not give him any food without checking with the doctor first. I half expect that in one of your next letters I will find a photo of little Ronny, and his other Oma would naturally also like to receive one. She visits me regularly and is now feeling a lot better*

22 Rosine - Bertha's niece's Eefke's young daughter.

*again. In her last letter she again wrote about Wally, who sent me a postcard this week, and I will write to her after I have finished this letter. She and Gunter have settled down and he attends the Froebel school*[23] *every day. Yesterday I surprised them together, with my niece Ida, by sending them some pretty tulips as at this time of year they are beautifully in bloom. Lotte will also be pleased with the note I sent with the flowers. Now the weather is slowly improving will you be taking Ronny out for walks? Does he have a nice pram? Erich are you speaking to your brother again or do you still not see each other? Please let me know as I am interested. All those who have had a birthday thank you for your good wishes. Oom Ies*[24] *has been in bed for the past three weeks and will have to stay in bed for another three weeks but this time it was not as bad as the previous attack. You must not say a word to Myra because she will be very worried. It is Gina's*[25] *birthday this month and like last year I will make a pretty dress for her doll. How are you Erich? Surely you are still working and does your little son let you have peaceful nights? Hanna you are not feeding the child at night any more - are you? How much does he weigh now? Please let me know. We have a little girl baby in the house where I live that is three days older than Ronny. She was born on the 25th October. Ronny is already four months old. How quickly time goes by and I would dearly like to see him, but with God's help that day will come. Hanna did you put on weight after the birth of the child and does Erich look like a proud father? If you speak to Myra make sure that you send her my regards. I will write to her again. Should Hans come to your home again please let him add a few words for Wally. That Eefke and little Rosine had visited Mother I have already related. Eefke's husband will be coming here next week for the annual trade fair. So my precious children I have written about everything to you and hope that I can look forward to hearing some good news from you. All the family and friends send their regards, including Dr Schweizer*

23 Friedrich Froebel school - a school based on his ideas which offered a holistic kindergarten and primary curriculum led by children's interests.

24 Oom Ies - Bertha's brother and the father to Sem and Myra.

25 Gina - Sem's young daughter.

*who comes here to visit as a guest. Erich you know him well. I wish you all the very best of health and all the very best and hope that you celebrate an enjoyable Easter. Best wishes and kisses from your ever-loving Moeke and Oma. And special regards for Hans, and also specially a lot of kisses for my little Ronny. I enclose an international pre-paid reply stamp and perhaps you can do the same. I will send a little present in your name on Oma's birthday.*

---

## April 1941

1 It becomes mandatory that signs have to be displayed at hotels, restaurants, cafes, zoos, art galleries, concert halls, libraries, theatres, cinemas and public meeting halls saying" Jews Prohibited" to re-enforce the decree made in January 1941 prohibiting Jews from entering any such premises.

1 Currency barriers between German and the Netherlands are removed.

2 Dutch Scouting associations dissolved by Germans.

10 Amsterdam Jews prohibited from moving out of the city.

11 Germans take over and now control the Jewish Weekly newspaper.

15 It was decreed that all Jews must surrender their radios within two weeks. To discourage vandalism the radios had to be in working order when handed in or the Jewish owner would have to pay the repair costs.

19 Milk is now rationed.

26 Potatoes are now rationed.

30 Images of the Dutch Royal family banned.

Although the process of issuing German identification cards to the whole Dutch population started in April it was not until the end of the year that this was completed.

## May 1941

1 Jewish lawyers, doctors, pharmacists, and translators not allowed to work for gentiles.
1 Jews banned from the Stock Exchange.
1 Jews banned from going to markets.
2 Jewish journalists laid off.
15 Nazis forbid any Jewish music to be played.
16 Dutch Actors Union closed down by Germans.
19 Use of bicycle taxis forbidden.
20 Decrees issued concerning the enforcement of public order.
28 Jewish owned farms had to be sold.
31 Jews no longer allowed to visit race tracks, tourist spots or use swimming pools or go onto public beaches.

---

*Dear Hanna and Erich and Hans* *5/5/41*

*Yesterday I visited Tante Tes and while I was there read a letter from Myra in which she told of the terrible news about your little darling. Words cannot express how awful I feel and I was so looking forward to seeing him, to kiss him, and to sitting him on my knee. But it seems that none of this is to be allowed us. Dear Hanna and Erich it is not my intention to again tear open the wound that the loss of your little darling caused with these words but to send you words of consolation to you in your grief. I imagine that as he was only seven months old that he was weak, and as Myra writes, had to have an operation. It is possible that he would have permanently remained a sickly child which might have been even harder for you both. The good Lord has embraced him and taken him to Himself and you are not able to counter his Will. Hanna do not think that your mother can easily cope with such an event? Although it is easy to write such things believe me when I tell you that it has made me ill and am not really in a state to write you a normal letter. In any case I send you my heartfelt condolences at your very sad loss (and also in the name of your step-father) and hope that dear God will protect you against further disasters and will also let you see the happier side of life. The two of you should be courageous and console each other. Erich console your wife because she needs your help and Hanna you should console him as his loss is as great as yours. In front of me I have the Biedermeier bonnet*[26] *to which I treated myself in his name and which I will always keep as a reminder. You would do me a great favour if you could let me have a photo of the little darling so that I can keep it with the Biedermeier bonnet so that I will always see him in front of me. Dear Hanna, according to what Erich has written, you were so brave during the birth and be brave now as should you Erich. It is the best advice that I or anyone else can give you. Tomorrow I will break the news as gently as possible to Oma, the other grandmother, lately he has been her topic of conversation. Oma and everyone else are all well and all send you greetings and kisses. Now something about yourselves. I hope that you are both in the best of health. Hanna why did you not add a few lines to Myra's letter to me? You can understand that I am keen to have any news. Since you wrote the letter telling me all about Ronny's birth I heard no more. Erich you are still working, as Hans wrote to me? Three weeks ago we had two letters from him and another one today. I am also writing to Wally today as I had a letter from her yesterday and she and Gunter are vey well. So dear Hanna and Erich I have run out of paper and I have to finish. Both of you should keep being strong and brave and especially be well. And please let me have some news from you very soon. Many heartfelt greetings and kisses for you both from your loving mother. In the names of the many relatives and friends that are here I have to send you their condolences. Thus Hanna and Erich look after yourselves and be well and let us hope that we can look forward to a speedy re-union.*

---

26 Biedermeier bonnet - very popular lades' headwear in the 19th century and is a straw bonnet with a wide front rim which has a tying ribbon at the base of the raised part.

Ronny died on 9th February 1941 being just over three months old of pyloric stenosis. (This is a narrowing of the opening from the stomach to the first part of the small intestine due to the enlargement of muscle at the opening. This condition occurs in one or two babies per 500 and is operable if correctly diagnosed.)

Bertha refers to Ronny being seven month old as she must have just heard the news about the loss of her grandchild in May. The following letter written five days later is very similar to the one above and illustrates the grief Bertha must have felt.

---

*Dear Hanna and Erich* *10/5/41*

*When I was at Oom Ies during the week I read a letter from Myra in which she mentioned some terrible news that your lovely little darling Ronny has been taken away from you and from us forever. I can imagine that it must have been a terrible shock for you both as he was always a large part of your happiness, but dear Hanna and Erich this should not have been allowed to happen. According to what Myra wrote he had to have an operation on his throat as he had difficulty swallowing and instead of him becoming a weak and poorly child the good Lord preferred to take him to Himself. You should both be consoled by this. One is not allowed and nor should one act against his Will. I hope that you will in future be protected from further catastrophes and that the good Lord will show you the better side of life. I am sure that I need not write how awful I, and all of us, found the news. I had set my heart on holding him and kissing him. To be a grandmother for the first time! That would have been lovely but it is made all the worse in that the joy was so short-lived and that I never saw him. You must have a photo of my little darling so please send it to me, especially as I have repeatedly already asked for it. I will tell the other grandmother who will also find the news terrible. Now something about you. I do hope that you have a positive outlook and that you are well. Dear Erich you should try to console Hanna as much as possible because that is what she needs now, and Hanna you should do the same. After a very long time Tante Ida came to visit me this week. She looked very well and asked that I send you her best wishes. Dear Hanna, before I forget, let me take this opportunity to congratulate you for your birthday, including Erich, and let us hope that we can celebrate the next one together. If you have received this letter from me you will have received the letter from Mr Klee*[27]*. Are they not wonderful people? Hanna and Erich if you write to Myra why do you not also drop me a line? I again send you both my condolences at the loss of your little darling also on behalf of your stepfather and all your family and friends. Hanna and Erich I expect to receive a letter from you very soon and tell me a lot about Ronny. Erich will ensure that she writes as she is a little tardy when it comes to writing. This week we had the third letter from Hans in which he wrote that he was well. I let Wally read them. If the weather is nice at Whitsun I will go and visit Wally. Well I will have to finish as the paper has come to an end. I wish you all the best, especially good health, and many heartfelt greetings and kisses from your loving mother. Hanna you were so brave during the birth of the baby and kept yourself so strong so do it again, and you Erich, and look forward to the day I will be seeing you again.*

---

### June 1941

1 All Catholic publications banned.
4 Further travel restrictions for Jews introduced.
11 Second large round-up of 300 Jews in Amsterdam who are sent to Mauthausen concentration camp.
18 Dutch are ordered to hand over their lead, copper, tin, nickel and other materials for recycling for the war effort. Many of the Dutch bury or hide such items that they have as an act of sabotage.

27 Mr Klee - the son of one of Bertha's friends in Amsterdam. He worked and lived in Geneva and was their postal intermediary.

26 All shops to be closed on Sundays.
27 Dutch Nazi Arnold Meyer leads demonstration against communists and Jews in Amsterdam.
30 Personal natural gas and electricity usage allocations restricted.

JULY 1941

3 Identity cards of Jews now stamped with a large "J".
5 Germans disband political parties.
14 Five people in Westmaas sentenced to death for helping Allied pilots.
14 Jews no longer allowed to be awarded academic degrees.
14 Jam is now rationed.
25 Jews prohibited from owning pigeons which might have been a source of un-rationed meat.
26 Austrian refugees forced to leave the Hague.

AUGUST 1941

6 Dutch police battalion allowed to seize Jews off the streets in Amsterdam.
8 By Decree 148 Jews were now ordered to deposit their cash, securities, stocks and bank accounts and holdings with Lippmann Rosenthal & Co to 'administer' their funds. Lippmann Rosenthal & Co was a bank set up and controlled by the Nazis who had chosen a Jewish sounding name to try to gain the confidence of the Jewish population. Jews were allowed to keep their wedding rings, pocket watches and dental fillings but were only allowed to withdraw up to 250 guilders a month per family of their seized assets for living expenses.
11 Employers organisations closed down by the Germans.
11 The Nazi created Dutch Estates Management Organisation which had the legal authority to seize or con-

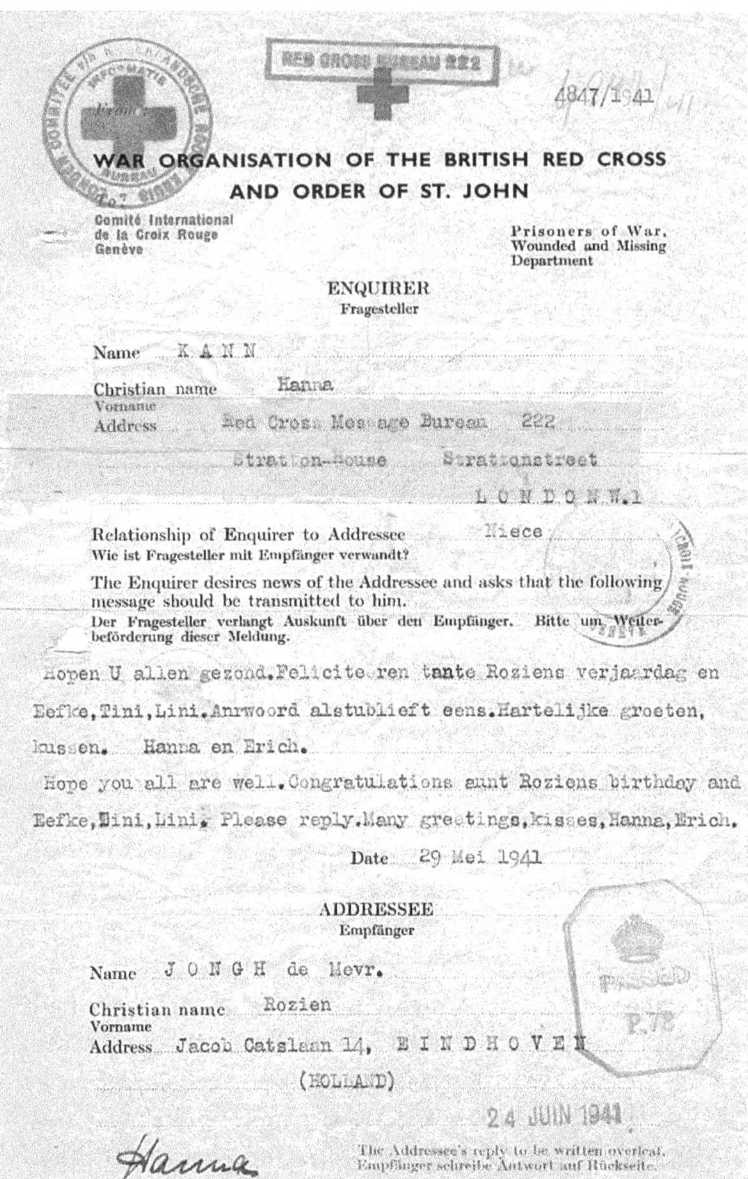

RED CROSS BUREAU 222

4847/1941

WAR ORGANISATION OF THE BRITISH RED CROSS
AND ORDER OF ST. JOHN

Comité International
de la Croix Rouge
Genève

Prisoners of War,
Wounded and Missing
Department

ENQUIRER
Fragesteller

Name K A N N

Christian name Hanna
Vorname

Address Red Cross Message Bureau 222
Stratton-House Strattonstreet
L O N D O N W.1

Relationship of Enquirer to Addressee Niece
Wie ist Fragesteller mit Empfänger verwandt?

The Enquirer desires news of the Addressee and asks that the following message should be transmitted to him.
Der Fragesteller verlangt Auskunft über den Empfänger. Bitte um Weiterbeförderung dieser Meldung.

Hopen U allen gezond.Feliciteeren tante Roziens verjaardag en Eefke,Tini,Lini.Anrwoord alstublieft eens.Hartelijke groeten, kussen. Hanna en Erich.

Hope you all are well.Congratulations aunt Roziens birthday and Eefke,Eini,Lini. Please reply.Many greetings,kisses,Hanna,Erich.

Date 29 Mei 1941

ADDRESSEE
Empfänger

Name J O N G H de Mevr.

Christian name Rozien
Vorname

Address Jacob Catslaan 14, E I N D H O V E N
(HOLLAND)

24 JUIN 1941

PASSED P.78

Hanna

The Addressee's reply to be written overleaf.
Empfänger schreibe Antwort auf Rückseite.

The translation of the Dutch into English is shown in the message.

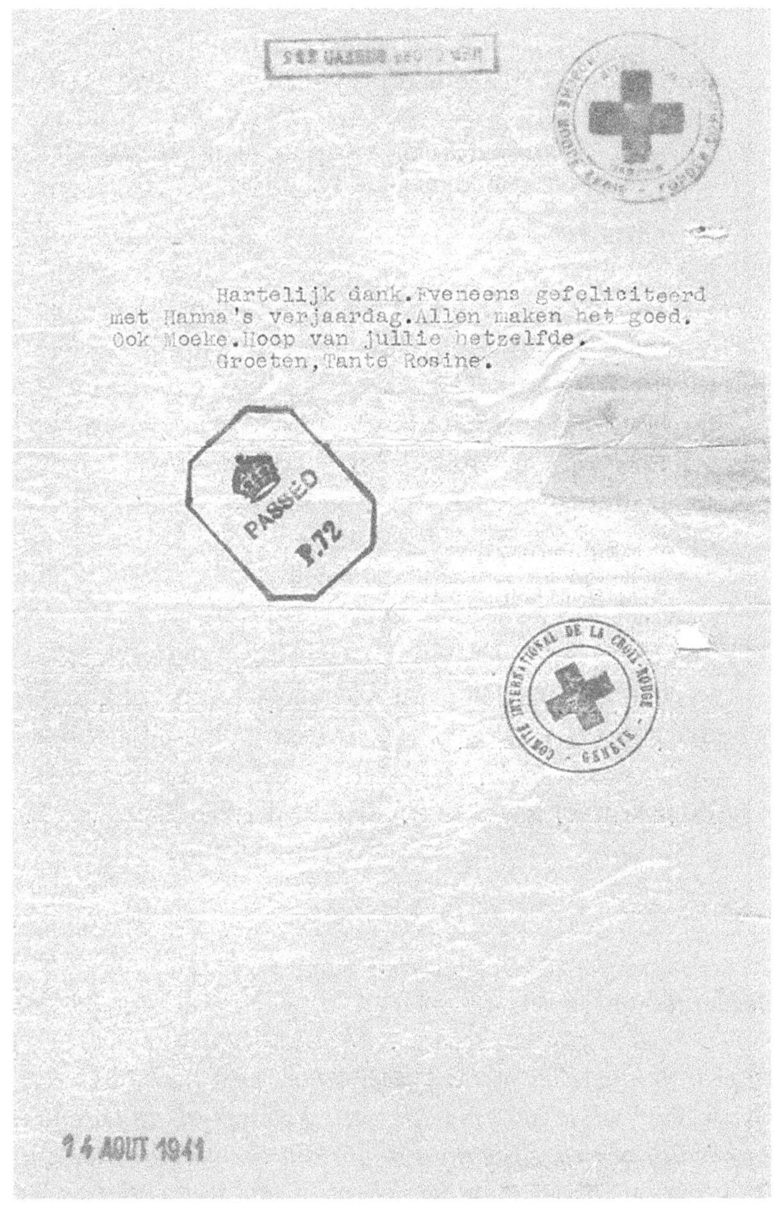

Hartelijk dank.Eveneens gefeliciteerd
met Hanna's verjaardag.Allen maken het goed.
Ook Moeke.Hoop van jullie hetzelfde.
Groeten,Tante Rosine.



The reply translates as - "Heartfelt thanks. Congratulations for Hanna's birthday. All are well. Also Moeke. Hope you are the same. Regards Tante Rosine.

fiscate Jewish assets, real estate, etc. or authorise non Jews to do so. These had previously been registered under Regulations 26/1940 and 48/1941.

18 German concentration camp at Amersfoort opened.

18 100 Jews rounded up in Gelderland who are arrested and then deported.

29 Jewish children could no longer be educated with Dutch children in public and vocational training schools. The children had to go to schools where they were educated by Jewish teachers, who had already been thrown out of work and prohibited from teaching in any Dutch school. Education was then supervised by the Jewish Council and financed by the funds confiscated from the Jews.

### September 1941

1 The Dutch and German currency becomes freely interchangeable so that the Germans could use their Reichmarks to purchase gold from the Dutch National Bank.

11 Round-up of Jews in Enschede and Twenthe.

16 All property belonging to Royalty confiscated.

---

*Dear Hanna and Erich* *28/9/41*

*I gather from the letter which I received on 23/9, the second day of the New Year[28], that you are both getting along well and are in the best of health, which is the most important thing at the moment. There is nothing better than being healthy and well and then, with a bit of luck, a person should be satisfied and content. I cannot say how very happy I was to get your letter this time especially as you both wrote so positively to me. I spent the other evening at Tante*

28 The Jewish New Year - this generally falls in September and is part of the High Holidays. It was then a two day celebration.

*Regina who asked me immediately when she saw me what had happened as you look different to usual. Well, you also know how it is if you are alone and on your own and have to face the world it can often be very forbidding but then when I get some news from you the world looks a different place . So you know that you can do me a favour by writing to me as much as possible. Now I am again waiting impatiently for news from you that the baby has arrived. Will it be a birthday present for you as Hanna writes? Keep an eye on her to make sure that she eats properly as otherwise she will not do it and she really needs to eat now. Tante Rosine did not receive a letter from you on her birthday but in any event she sends you both and Hans her regards and wishes you all the best and that all should be well in the future with you Hanna. Lini is expecting her third baby at the same time as you are. Tante Rosine is making a light blue coat with a cap for your baby - sounds nice. By coincidence both she and I happen to have sent Wally a parcel this week. Hans writes a lot and always includes your regards, please send him my regards. Yesterday I had a post card from Oma Ida and Oma Therese who both sent New Year's greetings. Oma[29] wrote that she is a lot better and Grete, Hans and Gisela are also well. She asked me to send her good wishes and kisses to you. I see from the menu that you have sent me that you are not short of anything and it is the same with me. Now I will let you know my menu for today - cauliflower soup, steamed cauliflower with potatoes and roast beef with a tasty gravy followed by steamed pears - not bad eh? The thing I do not like is being on my own. On Friday and Saturday nights I often go to visit one of my brothers and share a meal with them which is very enjoyable. Now I am happy that you have the cookbook to use with an electric oven and expect that you get on with it better than I could. For what I have to cook I do not need a cookbook. Use it to make something tasty. Of late I have been a frequent visitor at the Rosenzweigs and that is a whole change of scene for me. Lotte and specially Mrs Rosyn are very kind to me. I went there on the first day of the New Year for supper and they have asked me to*

29 Oma - this Oma (grandmother) is the mother of Erich and Hans who is living in Germany and mentions her daughter, son-in-law and granddaughter.

*break the fast with them on Yom Kippur*[30] *which I will do so that I will not be so alone on those days. You know that have not fasted the last few years but did fast last year. I did it for you as you were not able to. Again the situation is now the same and I will fast for you because this year you are definitely not able to fast and hope that you do not do so. In my last letter I forgot to send you greetings for the High Holidays*[31] *and do so now. I wish you many more healthy and happy years and that all your wishes may be fulfilled and especially you Hanna, that you may have a speedy confinement. As Hans visits you regularly and also reads your letters please pass on my good wishes to him. Do you still speak to Lini's brother in law or to Tante Carro's nephew? Last week I spoke to his mother Tante Nora who asked me to write to you that she has not had a letter from her son in a long time and wonders if he would write to her soon. I also hear that your friend Ro may soon be getting engaged as she walks arm in arm in public. I have also spoken to Reisel who said that she would like to add a few lines to my next letter to you. How nice that you like the work you started and that Erich is still working for the same firm as he is the breadwinner. You wrote that I should let you know a little about myself. I can write that I am well and that that is the most important thing at the moment. I am not as stout as I used to be. I lost a lot of weight when I heard the news of the loss of your little darling. Of late my appetite has returned and I am putting on weight again. The most important fact is that I am well. Erich I wish you many happy returns for your birthday and hope that you can celebrate many more together in health. I will write to you regularly and you should do the same because like you Hanna I also look at what the postman delivers and am disappointed if there is no news from you. Hanna I expect that you will write to me regularly so that I can be kept abreast of the news from you. In any event you must let me know directly when the baby has arrived. Oma is also wanting to know and Adele is here at the moment and sends you both her*

30 Yom Kippur - the Day of Atonement, the holiest day in the Jewish calendar marked with a 25 hour fast occurring during the High Holidays.

31 High Holidays - the period of Jewish festivals starting at the New Year and lasting several weeks, usually about September/October time.

*regards. Please congratulate Onkel Sem on his birthday. As I have brought you up to date on all the news I can now end my letter. I have just received a letter from Wally who writes that they are both well and she sends her regards. Oma Therese wrote asking that I include her best regards when writing to you and the same from all your family and the Rozenzweigs. Perhaps in your next letter you could mention them as they are very good to me. And now I wish you all the very best with heartfelt wishes and kisses from your ever loving mother. Moeke*
*Hanna make sure that you wear warm clothes.*

---

## October 1941

2 Non Jews not longer allowed to work as domestic help in Jewish homes.
3 RAF bomb Rotterdam harbour causing 106 casualties.
10 Forty little work camps set up for Jews in the Netherlands.
11 First NSB (Dutch Nazis) battalion departs for the Eastern Front to support the German Army.
20 Curtailment of Jews still working in professions.
20 All Jews in the Netherlands now to be recorded in a card index.
22 Aryans not longer allowed to work in Jewish retirement homes, hospitals, mental institutions, etc the exception being if working for an individual household if the maid is over fifty years of age and one of the employers is not Jewish.
22 Jews no longer allowed to be employed without a special work permit.
31 The authority of Amsterdam based Jewish Council now extended to cover all of the Netherlands. Jews living outside Amsterdam were only allowed to move to Amsterdam where most of the Dutch Jewish population lived.

RED CROSS BUREAU 222

13294/1941

From :

WAR ORGANISATION OF THE BRITISH RED CROSS AND ORDER OF ST. JOHN

To :

Comité International de la Croix Rouge Genève

Foreign Relations Department.

ENQUIRER
Fragesteller

Name K A N N

Christian name Hanna
Vorname

Address Red Cross Message Bureau 222
Stratton-House Strattonstreet
London W.1

Relationship of Enquirer to Addressee Mother
Wie ist Fragesteller mit Empfänger verwandt ?

The Enquirer desires news of the Addressee and asks that the following message should be transmitted to him.
Der Fragesteller verlangt Auskunft über den Empfänger. Bitte um Weiterbeförderung dieser Meldung.

Hoop U gezond. Is oom beter of ziekenhuis? Ben ongerust. Hier al en gezond. Heb geen post sinds Mei. Antwoord dadelijk. Kussen.

PASSED
P.74

Date 15 Oct. 1941

ADDRESSEE
Empfänger

Name J O R D A A N - B I E D E R M A N N

Christian name Bertha
Vorname

Address Zuider Amstellaan 16 II, A M S T E R D A M (Z)
(HOLLAND)

The Addressee's reply to be written overleaf. (Not more than 25 words).
Empfänger schreibe Antwort auf Rückseite. (Höchstzahl 25 worte).

15 OCT 1941

Hanna. 30 OCT. 1941

Message translates "Hope you are well. Is Oom better or in hospital. Am anxious. Here all well. Had no post since May. Answer by return. Kisses."

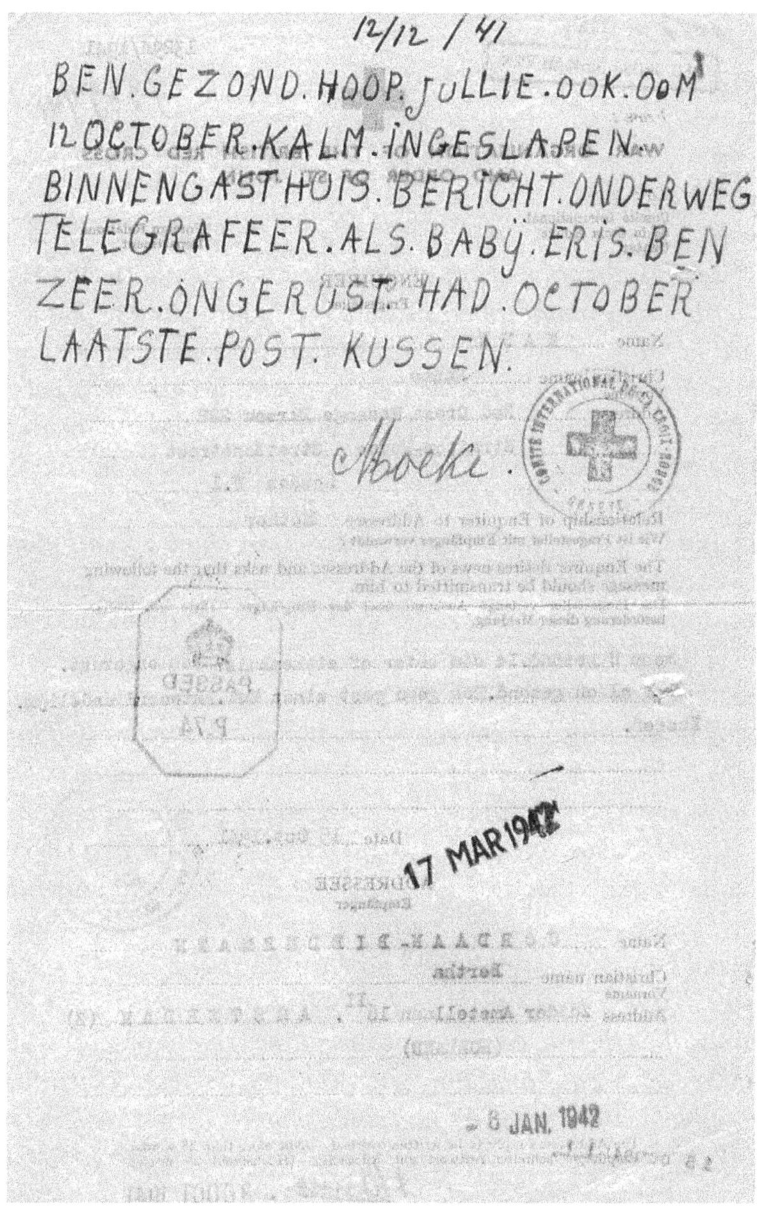

12/12/41
BEN.GEZOND.HOOP.JULLIE.OOK.OOM
12 OCTOBER.KALM.INGESLAPEN.
BINNENGASTHUIS.BERICHT.ONDERWEG
TELEGRAFEER.ALS.BABY.ERIS.BEN
ZEER.ONGERUST.HAD.OCTOBER
LAATSTE.POST.KUSSEN.

Moeke.

17 MAR 1942

6 JAN. 1942

Reply:"12/12/41 Am well. Hope you the same. Oom (one of the nicknames for Bertha's husband) peacefully fell asleep in hospice 12th October. News en route. Telegraph when baby arrives. Very anxious. Last post received October. Kisses."

*Dear Hanna and Erich* *27/10/41*

*Yesterday I received your letter of 30/9 in which you write about everything and that the baby is getting bigger. It is a great joy to receive such news and I suppose from that you two are also both well. This time I could cry tears of joy to have received your letter. Hanna you write nicely about things including that girl you met. Have you invited her to your home yet? What I find most amusing amongst your snippets of news is that you Hanna met this lady in the street and because of that you were able to buy such a reasonably priced comprehensive pretty baby layette. When I had to buy the outfits for little Gunter the clothes were also very reasonably priced. Will you write and let me know if you often hear from Hans and his mother as I would like to share such good news. Just before I started writing to you I spoke to Oma and conveyed to her your best wishes and kisses. I am very pleased that Erich has cared for Hanna so well that he has arranged that she will have the baby delivered in a private nursing home. This news gives me great peace of mind. I will be pleased to hear the news of the baby's birth as there will be one thing less to worry about.Hanna you are still writing about little Ronny and I suppose that you cannot forget a thing like that in a hurry, as I cannot. I still have in front of me the Biedermeyer bonnet that I bought in his name on my birthday. But with God's help if your other baby is fit and well he will slowly wear it out. Hanna it is good for you that you are going to carry on working as long as possible as you will be distracted and that cannot be a bad thing. In your letter you ask what I am doing with my time, regrettably nothing. It would be better for me if I had some hobbies or distractions. But I think that things will soon change as I am planning to go to help Tante Rosine run her household. For the time being she is all on her own and it is impossible for her to look after such a big house alone so that I will earn my keep. Now before I forget let me give you the recipe for the soup. Put some fat or butter, whatever you have handy, in the saucepan let it melt and then add some flour and stir continually with a wooden spoon until the colour of the flour is dark brown and the flour has become crumbly. Then add as much hot water as the amount of soup you want to make. Add a few bouillon cubes and taste before adding some salt and a very little amount of pepper, add a slice of old bread and if you happen to have an egg add that just before serving and it will add flavour. Good luck with your soup and bon appétit. You wrote that things are good between you and your husband and that he had preserved enough French beans for the winter. Shame that he was not here to help me so that Erich could have helped me to do some preserving but I had to do it all on my own. Oome also knew a bit about that. In the meantime Hanna you will have received your new skirt which should keep you nice and warm and hope that you will have a lot of pleasure in wearing it. You have asked about my health - Oh, as always sometimes it is better and sometimes my nerves are a bit worse. Some days I am out of sorts which I happen to be the day your letter arrived, but it cheered my up no end especially when I read that things are going well for you two. In the meantime have you found a new flat or have you decided to stay in your present flat? As you wrote you bought a new stove so it may be that you will be able to manage a little better. Myra writes home occasionally and Lex regularly write to Oom Tes. Sometimes he adds greetings for me but has never written a short note to me. Ask him if he can add a few words or write me a short note. How nice that Erich is still working for the same firm which should please you. Hanna you ask if Ro ever visits me, no I have not seen her for a very long time. Reisel has been here and I have been there a couple of times and in the evenings she walked me home. Reisel and her mother send you greetings and Reisel will add a few lines next time I write. You enquired about Lotte, she is not married. Lately I have enjoyed the company of Lotte and her mother. They are very kind to me and have invited me for dinner on several occasions which I accepted. Even more so in that she has been in hospital with bronchitis these last few weeks and I did not have any company. I visited her every day and three weeks ago I took a nice fruit bowl with me with a little card which said "With best wishes from Hanna and Erich". She was very pleased to receive it and ate up all the fruit wishing you both good health. She said that I should thank*

*you and send you her regards. Oome is better and no longer in hospital. When I write to you I often ask him to add a few lines. Hanna you know how lazy he is when it comes to writing and always says that if I write that will be alright. Every month I get news from Wally and they both seem well. I wrote to her yesterday and included greetings from you both and Hans. When you speak to Hans please make sure that you pass on my regards and tell him that he should write to me as I have not had any news from him for a long time. Well Hanna and Erich I brought you up to date with all the latest news here and hope that I will soon receive a very full letter from you with all good news. Hanna I would love you to see all the things that I knitted for the baby. So Hanna and Erich if you want to know a great big favour you could do for me it is to write to me as often as possible. Do not notice my bad handwriting and spelling mistakes as this will improve in time. I am going to end now as I have to save something for the next letter which I will write in a fortnight together with Tante Rosine. I wish you both the very best but specially for you Hanna that when the time comes with God's help you should have a good confinement and a strong and healthy baby. And with heartfelt love and large kisses your ever loving Moeke.*
*All members of our family and many friends all send you greetings. Especially from Lotte her mother and Julie.*

---

NOVEMBER 1941

1 Registry for Textiles withdraws permits from 1,600 Jewish merchants.
1 Jews no longer allowed to be members of an all Jewish organisation.
7 Jews no longer allowed to travel except with permit.
25 German citizenship revoked for all Jews not living in Germany. 30,000 Jews from Germany were resident in the Netherlands.

*Dear Hanna and Erich* *28/11/41*

*Although I heard no more after the letter in which you described the baby's outfit I thought that I would let you hear some of my news, in the hope that you are both well when you receive this letter. How are you both, especially you Hanna? By the time you receive this letter the baby may have already arrived. Will it be a birthday present for Erich? Hanna you are surely not working anymore. Have you found a suitable flat in the meantime or are you going to stay where you are? I think that the latter option is the better specially in the winter. And as Erich writes that you have a large stove the baby will not be cold. I have been at Tante Rosine for the last 14 days and am going home next Friday 20/11.*[32] *It is nice to be away and have a break from the humdrum. I do not know why but this time I do not have a lot to write to you about. If I had had a letter from you I would read it carefully and answer all the subjects brought up. This week I had a letter from Oma Therese and a postcard from my niece Ida. All are very well and send you both and Hans greetings and special kisses from Oma Ida. Erich, before I forget, I would like to send you greetings for your birthday to you and Hanna. I hope that you will be able to enjoy celebrating it together and that next time you will be able to celebrate with the whole family and that your perfect little son or daughter will arrive on your birthday. You will have to wait a while for the little birthday present from me but you can have the pleasure of looking forward to receiving it. In any case I will drink a nice cup of coffee to toast you on your birthday. I also had a letter from Wally this week who seems to be in good spirits and sends you and Hans regards. I would like to go and visit her and she would be very happy if I did so. I will reflect a little on the idea. I have not heard from Hans in a long time. I used to get 2 or 3 letters a week from him but now I do not hear anything. Give him my regards when you see him. Hanna you will be pleased when the baby arrives as towards the end of a pregnancy things can get a little difficult. I will also be*

32 Next Friday 20/11 - there seems to be a dating oversight as the letter is dated 28/11/41.

*pleased when it has ended and receive news that you and the child are well. You have chosen a good time for bed rest. Tante Esther has also been in bed the last few weeks, it is the same complaint as usual, her heart. Tante Regina also had a small operation on her eye but that is now completely healed. Pass on my regards to Innes and her parents. As Tante Rosine wants to write a few lines I will finish for today and write to you when I get home which will be next week. I look forward to soon receiving a long letter form you with lots of good news because as I wrote in my last letter this is the best way to console me. So again best wishes for your birthday and enjoy it together. Pass on my regards to Onkel Sem and his wife. I wish you the very very best confinement and many heartfelt wishes and kisses for you both from your ever loving Moeke.*
*Make sure that you remember me to Lex when you see him. I am making a couple of pretty stuffed animals out of oil-cloth for the expected baby. I think you know what I am talking about Hanna. I will write to Wally straight away and send her your best wishes on your behalf.*

*Dear Hanna, Erich*

*As Moeke is here it is a good opportunity to write to you. It gives me great pleasure to know that you are doing so well and that your family will increase with the arrival of a baby. Lini is expecting at the same time which is nice. I hope that everything will go quickly and well and that the baby will bring you much joy. Here all is well. We have regular news from Eefke and her family and the other children are well. That is all the news that I have at the moment.*
*Keep well and regards from Oom Sam and me and a big kiss for Hanna from Tante Rosine.*
*ps I have a blue coat and cap for the baby.*

---

DECEMBER 1941

5 All non Dutch Jews ordered to register for 'voluntary emigration'.
14 Germans dissolve the National Front, NSNAP and National Union organisations. NSB becomes the only political party. Students forced to join NAD.
15 Further restrictions of gas and electricity supplies.
17 Dutch Reformed Churches protest against labour conscription.
30 Dutch physicians required to join Nazi doctor's union.

Unfortunately over half of the following letter cannot be read as the ink has faded.

---

*Dear Hanna and Erich* *8/12/41*

*As I have not heard from you for a while (the letter in which you describe the baby's layette) I will write again hoping that this letter finds you in the best of health. I hope and wonder if your baby has arrived. You can well imagine how urgently I await that news from you. Hanna and Erich why are you so slow at writing letters? It is the only thing at the moment that keeps me going. In my last letter I mentioned that I spent 14 days with Tante Rosine and that the visit finished a week ago. Yesterday I spoke to the mother of ...* [the ink in the next section of the letter has largely faded, but the letter continues where readable] ... *I regularly receive post from Wally and they are well. I sent a parcel for St Nicholas for Gunter and included a birthday present for Wally. Oma is doing well and I have just written to her. Erich I am burning with curiosity if you will get a son or a daughter on your birthday. This time I only have a little bit of material to make something and will not do so until later. I hope to hear from you very soon. I wish you all the very best and a strong and healthy baby from which we may all have much joy.*

*Heartfelt greetings and kisses from your ever loving Moeke.*
*All family and friends also send their regards.*
*Many happy returns, have a good birthday and a prosperous 1942!!*

---

JANUARY 1942

10 Forced labour camps for Jews established in the north and west of the Netherlands.
14 Jews from Zaandam forced to move to Amsterdam.
14 Stateless Jews to report directly to Westerbork - a holding location before being sent East to be resettled (murdered).
27 Coldest day in the Netherlands since 1850 - temperatures down to -27.4C or -19F. Movement of Jews is restricted and they can now only live in Amsterdam.

---

*Dear Hanna Erich Hans and my little treasure* *25 January 1942*

*Firstly I would like to congratulate you on the birth of your baby. You can imagine how happy I was to receive the news from you. Especially when I heard that you Hanna and the baby are well and naturally Erich as well. I also told the Oma who was also delighted and sends you all her congratulations and best wishes. I think that Wally will come to visit me next week. In the meantime you will have heard from Oma. In another letter I will write a little more about that. Hanna surely you are feeding the child yourself. Do not go out while it is so cold and take care of him so that nothing happens to him. The baby is your first priority and you should drop everything to look after the baby and I think that Erich will also help take care of the baby. I can imagine how happy you both must be now that you have a baby again. From what you write it seems that all went well, and the baby weighs seven pounds*[33]*, which seems rather heavy for Hanna. And how does Hans feel now that he is an uncle again? Wally sends both you and him good wishes and congratulations. Why do you always write such short letters as I am always curious to hear something good from you. Hanna write and let me know how long you were in hospital. Erich do me a great favour and let me have a photo of your baby. It was my birthday last week and even Oma came to wish me a happy birthday. I will finish now because I want to write again next week. I hope that I will soon receive a letter from you with loads of good news and do not forget to write about the baby. Tante Rosine and the rest of the family also send their congratulations and best wishes. Regards to Hans and kisses from your loving mother and all the very best for your baby. A thousand kisses from Oma Bertha and Oma Ida for the baby. Lini was also delivered of a fine boy of six and a half pounds. Mother and child are well and he is called Jacky.*[34] *Will you also let Herman know when you speak to him. Once more affectionate wishes from mother.*

---

FEBRUARY 1942

18 Dutch actors protest at compulsory membership of Cultural Chamber.

MARCH 1942

13 Coffee substitute now rationed.

18 Members of the illegal 'Free Netherlanders' boycott theatres.

20 Jewish owned motor vehicles seized and Jews no longer allowed to ride in motor cars with the exception of riding in an ambulances or a hearse or involved with war work.

33 The Dutch pound is half a kilo or 500 grams so that in fact the weight is just under seven and three quarter English pounds.

34 Jacky was exactly a week older than Ray and both grew up to be lifelong friends.

20 Jews prohibited to have sexual contact with non Jews.
20 Those of African origin forbidden to have sexual contact with Aryans.
25 Jews no longer allowed to marry non-Jews.
26 Forbidden to move furniture out of Jewish homes with the exception of the monopoly held by Abraham Puls & Sons, the Nazi-directed notorious Amsterdam moving-van company, employed to pillage Jewish homes.
26 The Nazi censored 'Jewish Weekly' containing anti-Jewish regulations was the only publication that Jews were allowed to publish.

---

*Dear Hanna Erich and Hans and my little treasure* *21/3/42*

*Yesterday I received your letter of 10/2 and am pleased to hear that you are all well which is most important to me as at the moment, good health is to be valued above all. I got your telegram about the baby's birth and thought he was born on January 1st but now that I have read your letter I see it is 31st December. I appreciate that you wrote to let me know about the whole confinement. You are quite right in that you thought that I would be very interested. I can imagine how happy you two are with the birth of the new baby. I also thank you Erich that you cared for Hanna during her pregnancy and the delivery and hope soon to thank you personally. When I received your news I immediately let Oma know, who was very pleased when she heard, and naturally I also let Wally know. I will see Oma tomorrow and will show her your letter. Last time I spoke to her she was very well. How nice Hanna that you were given so much for the baby but nothing yet from Opoe[35], but that will come. Erich will you mention it to him but as Hanna writes you make a nice family photo. Hans is probably pleased that you are good friends again and that he can often visit you. It is much better like this. Send him my regards and especially those from Wally and Gunter who are both well. I think that Wally will come to stay with me for a few days next month and we will have a lot to talk about. Erich make sure that Hanna gets enough to eat and drink as otherwise your son will not get enough nutrition. Papa Erich will surely have taken a photograph of him and I am already looking forward to my joy at receiving this with your next letter. As he gets to know his family by his photograph so his family will meet him. I expect that you received the letter I wrote about the passing of Oome*[35]*. Now I want to tell you the course of the illness. While Hanna was pregnant I did not want her to know and in my last letter (in which Rosine added a few words) that Oome was no longer poorly, which was indeed the case, as he had been dead for a few months. On 19 May I went with Oome by tram to hospital where he was to stay for observation for his bronchitis (I wrote that we went by tram so you would not think that he was very ill). The first week I visited him three times but then I visited him every day as the doctor had said that he had chronic inflammation of the lungs. After a few weeks I spoke to the doctor personally who took me to his consulting room and told me that he had to speak to me very seriously and said "Madam your husband has lung cancer which is probably incurable." I then visited him twice a day. On 7th July I baked something special for him and also took him a thermos of coffee and cream and together we celebrated your birthday in the hospital which he enjoyed and was a surprise as he did not know that I was coming to visit him that afternoon. I had asked the matron beforehand if this would be allowed. So from 19th May to 12 October (when he died) is exactly the 20 weeks that he was in hospital. He had a lot of pain except for the last few days when he was no longer conscious but calm and quietly died in his sleep. You can imagine how weary I was after 20 weeks of going to the hospital once or twice a day. Naturally I also suffered but hope that I will soon get over it. So as not to be so alone I want to go to Tante Rosine. Due to various circumstances this was not possible so I had to stay at home. Also Oom Jul*[36] *had been in*

35 Opoe/Oome were both nicknames of Bertha's second husband.

36 Jul was one of Bertha's brothers.

*hospital for a couple of days and died on 12 September which is exactly five weeks before Oome was buried. Hanna and Erich although this happened half a year ago you should put this behind you as soon as possible. Why is it that you take so long to reply as I am always waiting impatiently for your next letter as this is all that I have to look forward to. I am sure that you understand. I was expecting a letter from you for some time as I had not received anything for my birthday. Hanna you wrote that you had sent me good wishes for my birthday in an earlier letter but I did not receive it. I only got your good wishes in your last letter. Hanna let me know if you have put on any weight after the birth of the baby. How nice that you two will be able to go for walks with your son and uncle Hans will also probably join you. When Wally comes to visit me we will write a letter together. Oh yes Hanna I wanted to let you know that Lini had a dear little boy on 24 December called Jacky. If you see her brother-in-law please let him know. I think that it is Hans' birthday this month so please send him my best wishes and hope that he can celebrate his next birthday with his wife and son. I still have to congratulate Oma Ida whose birthday it is this week. I will have to finish now as I have written everything about everything that I know. I am presently helping Oom Karel*[37] *because his wife has been in hospital for several weeks but is coming home this week. Then I can go to my home for which I am rather thankful as it is very busy here, far too busy for my liking. Oh yes there is some news that I must give you that I have not mentioned yet which is that Tini is getting married on 1st April, and it is not an April Fool's joke but for real. She told her parents last Tuesday and they were not cross at hearing the news. Now dear children I really have to finish because the page is full and will write to you again in a fortnight and hope that I will very soon hear good news about you all, and specially my little treasure, and look forward to receiving a photo of him with his mummy and daddy. Best wishes for you all, with loving kisses form your everloving mother and Opoe, with a special kiss for Ray and a big kiss for Hans.*

*Don't be so mean with the stamps and write more often. I am always waiting for your letters. All family and friends send their best*

37 Karel was another brother of Bertha.

*wishes especially Oma, Grete, Hans, Gisela, Wally and Gunter, and a special kiss for Ray.*
*ps*
*Just now Oma Ida came by and asked me to congratulate you on the birth of the baby.*

---

APRIL 1942

1 Jews no longer allowed to marry in the Amsterdam town hall.
1 Compulsory labour subscription.
1 First deportation of Jewish hospital patients.
10 Sweets, chocolates and cigarettes are now rationed.
20 Dutch people no longer allowed access to beaches.
24 Most Jewish butchers shops have to close.
29 Jews over six years of age were forced to wear a yellow star the size of a hand with the word 'Jew' printed on it sewn onto clothes which covered their left breast.
30 Jews not allowed to be members of the only trade union.

MAY 1942

1 Radio Orange calls for Jews to defy order for wearing the yellow star.
4 450 prominent Dutchmen taken as hostages by the German occupiers.
15 2,000 Netherlands Army officers arrested and taken to Germany.
17 Dutch SS members vow their personal loyalty to Hitler.
21 Accountancy, pharmacy and pawn broking amongst occupations closed to Jews.
21 Jews had to register their bicycles, with the exception of those who worked for the Jewish Council or have special permission to use a bicycle.
21 Jews obliged to hand in their gold, silver, antiques,

RED CROSS BUREAU 222

From :

19493/42

**WAR ORGANISATION OF THE BRITISH RED CROSS AND ORDER OF ST. JOHN**

To :

Comité International
de la Croix Rouge
Genève

Foreign Relations Department.

PASSED P.74

ENQUIRER
Fragesteller

Name K A N N.

Christian name Hanna.
Vorname

Address RED CROSS MESSAGE BUREAU 222.
STRATTON HOUSE STRATTON STREET
LONDON W.1.

Relationship of Enquirer to Addressee Daughter.
Wie ist Fragesteller mit Empfänger verwandt ?

The Enquirer desires news of the Addressee and asks that the following message should be transmitted to him.
Der Fragesteller verlangt Auskunft über den Empfänger. Bitte um Weiterbeförderung dieser Meldung.

HOPEN U GEZOND, ZOOALS WIJ. RAY GROEIT GOED PROBEERT TE ZITTEN, BERICHTEN ONDERWEG. HOOP ALLES ONTVANGEN. SCHRIJF ALSTUBLIEFT GEREGELD ANDERS ONGERUST. HARTELIJKE KUSSEN VOOR OPOETJE.

Date 9-6-42.

Hanna, Eric, Ray.

ADDRESSEE
Empfänger

Name J O R D A A N - B I E D E R M A N N.

Christian name Bertha.
Vorname

Address Zuider Amstellaan 16 II
A M S T E R D A M (Z) (NH)
NEDERLAND.

The Addressee's reply to be written overleaf. (Not more than 25 words).
Empfänger schreibe Antwort auf Rückseite. (Höchstzahl 25 worte).

28 JUIN 1942

"Hope you are well as we are. Ray grows well tries to sit. News on the way. Hope all received. Please write regularly as otherwise anxious. Fond kisses for Opoetje."

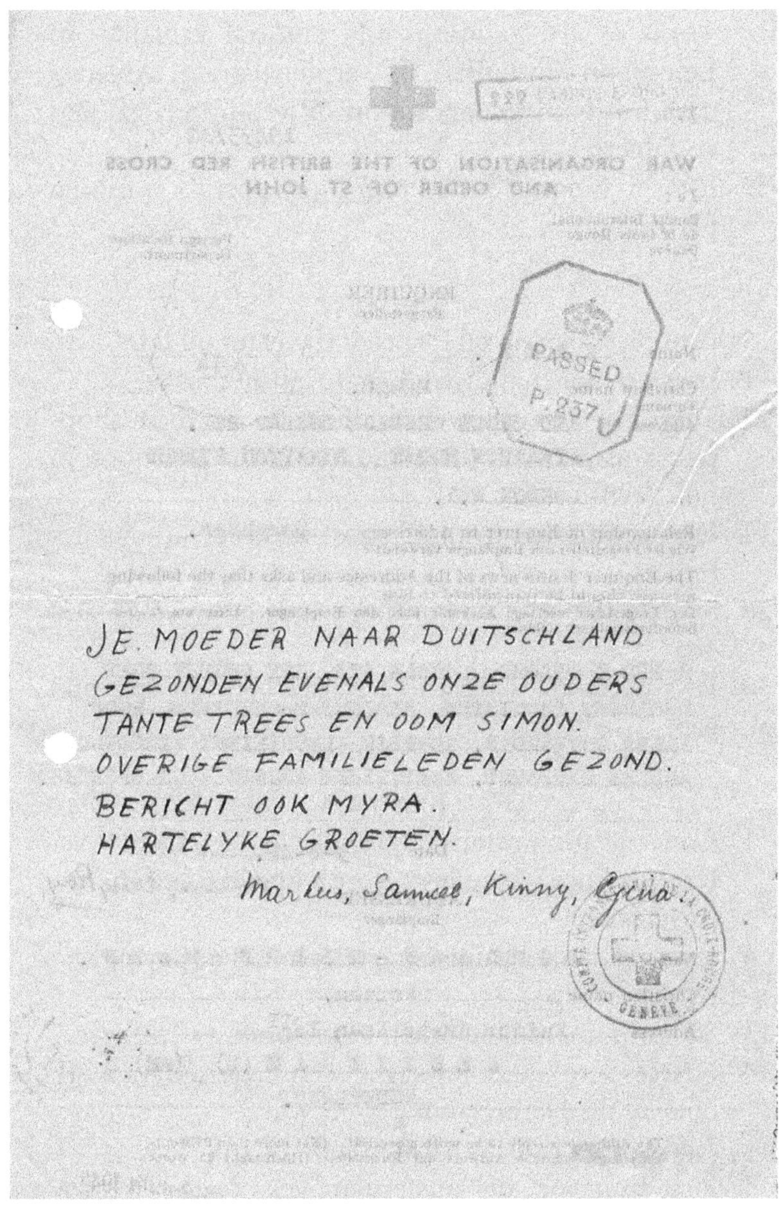

JE MOEDER NAAR DUITSCHLAND
GEZONDEN EVENALS ONZE OUDERS
TANTE TREES EN OOM SIMON.
OVERIGE FAMILIELEDEN GEZOND.
BERICHT OOK MYRA.
HARTELYKE GROETEN.

Markus, Samuel, Kinny, Gina

PASSED
P. 237

Reply reads: "Your mother sent to Germany as our parents, Auntie Trees and Uncle Simon. Remainder of family well. Let Myra know. Affectionate greetings."

works of art, paintings and cultural valuables to Lippmann Rosenthal in Sarphartistraat, Amsterdam but with the exception of wedding rings and gold teeth.

29 Jews no longer allowed to fish or apply for a fishing permit.

### June 1942

5 Complete ban on all forms of travel for all Jews.

11 Jews no longer allowed to go to a fish market.

12 The only time allowed for Jews to do their shopping was between three and five in the afternoon in non-Jewish shops.

14 Jews prohibited from all sport and recreational activities.

26 Start of deportations of those aged between 16 and 40.

30 Jews were now subject to a curfew between 8pm and 6am.

### July 1942

1 Concentration camps established at Vught and Westerbork from where Jews were shipped to, primarily, Auschwitz.

6 Jews prohibited from using telephones or paying visits to non Jews.

13 800 prominent Dutchmen imprisoned as hostages.

14 Notices sent out to Jews who were required for work outside the Netherlands.

14 Anti Jewish riots in Amsterdam.

14 First transport of Amsterdam Jews to the Westerbork transit camp.

15 First train with 1,135 Jews leaves Westerbork for Auschwitz. Transports will continue every Tuesday morning to Auschwitz or Sobibor until 3rd September 1944. Almost nobody survives.

19 Bicycles confiscated by the Germans in Rotterdam and the Hague.
21 Jews in Amsterdam have to hand in their bicycles by this date.
22 The Amsterdam Jewish theatre 'Hollandsche Schouwburg' requisitioned as the reporting place for Jews and where arrested and 'discovered' Jews are held.
26 Roman Catholic churches and bishops join protests at the spread of Judaism.
30 Throughout the Netherlands 722 Catholics of Jewish descent were listed.
31 Jews no longer allowed to go to hairdressers.

AUGUST 1942

1 Names of all Dutch telephone subscribers required by the Germans.
2 250 Dutch Catholics of Jewish descent arrested and transported to Amersfoort camp.
6-8 Riots by Dutch Jews.
9 All Jewish street names are removed and changed.
7 Dutch resistance bombs Rotterdam railway.
25 SS start deporting Jews from Maastricht.

SEPTEMBER 1942

8 Jews no longer allowed to sit on public benches in The Hague.
15 Jewish pupils no longer allowed to attend school.

OCTOBER 1942

1 Jews in Dutch labour camps transferred to Westerbork.
15 Jewish children separated from their parents when they arrive at the holding location of Hollandsche Schouwburg theatre in Amsterdam and then kept in a crèche across the road to be deported separately from adults.

Dit bericht gaat naar
Dochter en Man.

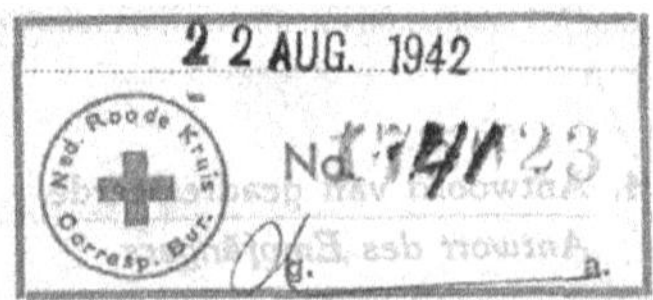


Het Nederlandsche Roode Kruis

Formulier, na invulling, in te zenden aan het *CORRESPONDENTIE-BUREAU* van het Nederlandsche Roode Kruis, Carel van Bylandtlaan 10, Den Haag.

VERZOEK
door tusschenkomst van het Duitsche Roode Kruis aan het Internationale Comité van het Roode Kruis te Genève om inlichtingen.

*ANTRAG*
*durch das Deutsche Rote Kreuz an das Internationale Komitee vom Roten Kreuz in Genf auf Nachrichtenvermittlung*

1. Afzender B. JORDAAN.
*Absender* (naam, voornaam en adres)
*(Name, Taufname und Adresse)*

16 ZUIDER. AMSTELLAAN. 16 II AMSTERDAM.

Verzoekt aan
*Bittet an*

2. Geadresseerde E. KANN. GROST.
*Empfänger* (naam, voornaam en adres)
*(Name, Taufname und Adresse)*

28. HEMSTAL. ROAD 28. LONDEN. N.W.6.

het volgende mede te deelen:
*folgendes zu übermitteln:*

(ten hoogste 25 woorden uitsluitend persoonlijke en familieaangelegenheden betreffende)
*(Höchstzahl 25 Worte nur persönliche und Familienangelegenheiten betreffend)*

HOOP. JULLIE. ALLEN. GEZOND. EVENALS. IK.
IK. SCHRIJF. REGELMATIG. SEDERT. JUNI.
GEEN. BERICHT. BEN. ZEER. ONGERUST.
GROEIT. BABY. FLINK. ANTWOORD. DIRECT.
HARTELIJKE. KUSSEN. MOEKE. OPOETJE.

Handteekening
*Unterschrift*

3. Geadresseerde antwoordt aan ommezijde
*Empfänger antwortet umseitig*

16 Augustus 1942

B. Jordaan

At the top: "This message is for my daughter and husband". The enquiry by Hanna's mother reads: "Hope that you are all well as I am. Write regularly. No news since June. Very anxious. Is baby growing well. Reply immediately. Loving kisses Moeke Opoetje."

This is the first page of one of the letters Hanna wrote to her mother dated 22 October, 29 October, 5 November and 12 November that returned to Hanna as her mother was no longer living at the address. (Possibly the numbers in the top left hand corner are censor references.)

As with all the letters this is typically very closely written on Air Mail paper which is very thin so that the writing on the reverse side comes through and makes it difficult to read. Erich worked in a retail shop that closed early on a Thursday, when the letters were written.

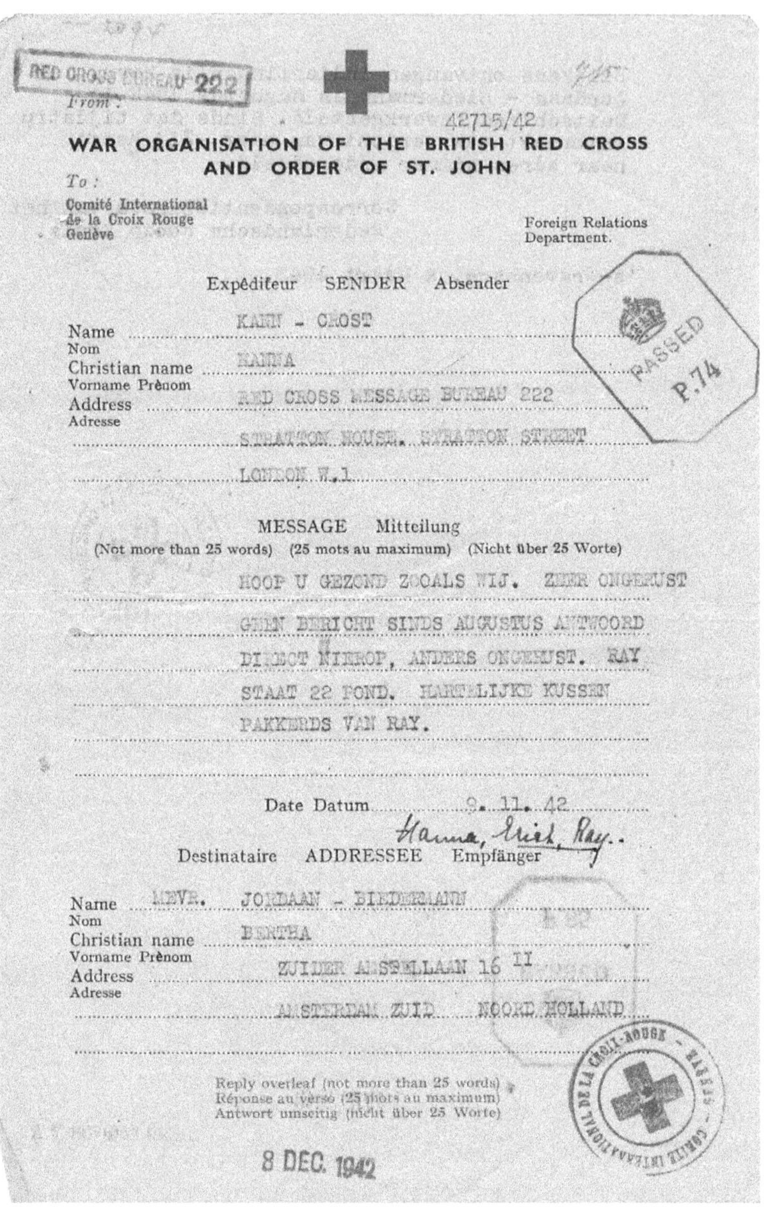

RED CROSS BUREAU 222

From:

42715/42

WAR ORGANISATION OF THE BRITISH RED CROSS AND ORDER OF ST. JOHN

To:

Comité International de la Croix Rouge Genève

Foreign Relations Department.

PASSED P.74

Expéditeur SENDER Absender

Name / Nom: KAHN - CROST

Christian name / Vorname Prénom: HANNA

Address / Adresse: RED CROSS MESSAGE BUREAU 222 STRATTON HOUSE, STRATTON STREET LONDON W.1

MESSAGE Mitteilung

(Not more than 25 words) (25 mots au maximum) (Nicht über 25 Worte)

HOOP U GEZOND ZOOALS WIJ. ZEER ONGERUST GEEN BERICHT SINDS AUGUSTUS ANTWOORD DIRECT NIEROP, ANDERS ONGERUST. RAY STAAT 22 POND. HARTELIJKE KUSSEN PAKKERDS VAN RAY.

Date Datum: 9. 11. 42

Hanna, Erich, Ray.

Destinataire ADDRESSEE Empfänger

Name / Nom: MEVR. JORDAAN - BIEDERMANN

Christian name / Vorname Prénom: BERTHA

Address / Adresse: ZUIDER AMSTELLAAN 16 II AMSTERDAM ZUID NOORD HOLLAND

Reply overleaf (not more than 25 words)
Réponse au verso (25 mots au maximum)
Antwort umseitig (nicht über 25 Worte)

8 DEC. 1942

COMITÉ INTERNATIONAL DE LA CROIX-ROUGE GENÈVE

Message reads: "Hope that you are well as we are. Very worried no news since August. Reply immediately as otherwise even more worried. Ray weighs 22 pounds. Fond kiss and hugs from Ray."

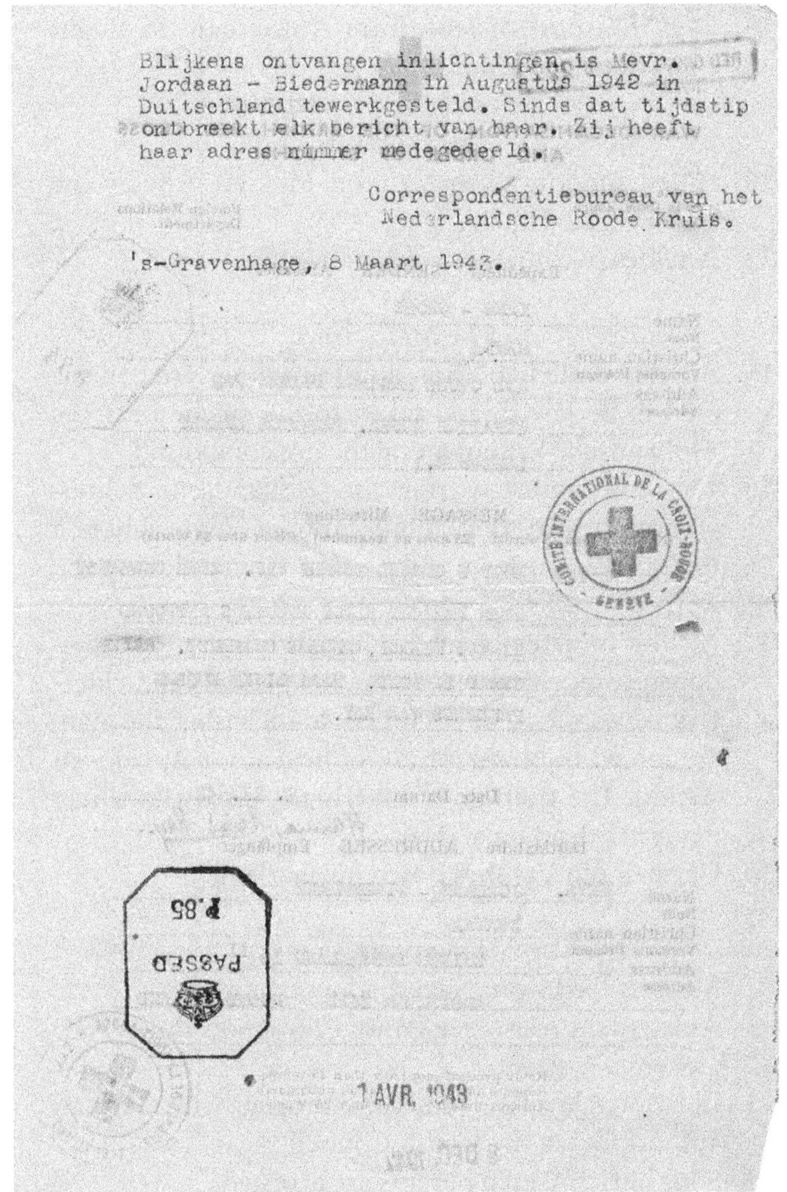
Blijkens ontvangen inlichtingen is Mevr. Jordaan - Biedermann in Augustus 1942 in Duitschland tewerkgesteld. Sinds dat tijdstip ontbreekt elk bericht van haar. Zij heeft haar adres nimmer medegedeeld.

Correspondentiebureau van het Nederlandsche Roode Kruis.

's-Gravenhage, 8 Maart 1943.



"According to reports received Mrs Jordaan - Biedermann went to Germany to work in August 1942. Since that time no reports about her have been received. She failed to communicate her new address. Correspondence office of the Dutch Red Cross. The Hague 8 March 1943."

15 First transport of Jews from Amsterdam to Vught concentration camp.

### December 1942

10 Hitler announces that Anton Mussert will be the leader of the Dutch people.

31 Potatoes become subject to rationing.

### January 1943

15 All abandoned children and foundlings are considered to be Jewish and taken to the crèche near the 'Hollandsche Schouwburg' theatre compound.

16 450 Jews deported from the 'Hollandsche Schouwburg' theatre to a labour camp at Vught where a total of 12,000 Jews will be imprisoned during the war.

21/22 All the inmates of in the Jewish home near Apeldoorn comprising Jewish mental patients and elderly folk, about 1250/1300 people including the staff, are forced to board a train of boxcars at Apeldoorn station. The train goes directly to Auschwitz where many are dead on arrival.

30 German officers shot down in Haarlem.

### February 1943

1 Mussert forms pro Nazi shadow cabinet.

5 Amsterdam resistance group CS6 shoots down Nazi General Seyffardt.

5 Individual Jews can only communicate with German authorities via the Jewish Council.

9 Sons of rich Dutch parents are arrested.

10 Another resistance group starts a fire in an Amsterdam employment bureau.

17 Dutch churches protest at the persecution of the Jews.

18 First edition of Dutch resistance newspaper 'Trouw' issued.

LONDON COMMITTEE OF
THE NETHERLAND RED CROSS SOCIETY

PRESIDENT:
H. R. H. PRINCESS JULIANA.
CHAIRMAN:
JONKHEER O.C.A. VAN LIDTH DE JEUDE.

Hon. Secretary:
JONKHEER A.P.C. VAN KARNEBEEK.
Hon. Treasurer:
J. TEN DOESSCHATE.
Bankers:
B. W. BLYDENSTEIN & Co.
54/56, THREADNEEDLE STREET, LONDON, E.C.2.

~~21A, PORTMAN SQUARE,~~
~~LONDON, W.1~~
Kindly reply to
The Secretary,
W. FRIEDHOFF,
120, PALL MALL, S.W.1.
Tel. ABBEY 2117.

C/PS.

5th February 1943.

Mrs.H.Kann.
28, Hemstal Road,
N.W.6.

Dear Madam,

We have been advised by our Lisbon Delegate that the parcel addressed on your behalf to Mevr.Jordaan-Bierman, Zd.Amstellaan 16, Amst erdam, (which name was included in our May 1942 list), has been returned owing to the addressee having gone away without leaving a new address.

Please advise me to whom we should now re-deliver the parcel.

Yours faithfully,

Friedhoff

First Red Cross letter

LONDON COMMITTEE OF

THE NETHERLAND RED CROSS SOCIETY

PRESIDENT:
H. R. H. PRINCESS JULIANA.

CHAIRMAN:
JONKHEER O.C.A. VAN LIDTH DE JEUDE.

Hon. Secretary:
JONKHEER A.P.C. VAN KARNEBEEK.

Hon. Treasurer:
J. TEN DOESSCHATE.

Bankers:
B. W. BLYDENSTEIN & Co.
54/56, THREADNEEDLE STREET, LONDON, E.C.2.

~~21a, PORTMAN SQUARE,~~
~~LONDON, W.1~~

Kindly reply to
The Secretary,
W. FRIEDHOFF,
120, PALL MALL, S.W.1.
Tel. ABBEY 2117.

C/RB

24th February, 1943.

Mrs. H. Kann,
28, Hemstal Road,
London. N.W. 6.

Dear Madam,

We have been advised by our Lisbon Delegate that a second parcel addressed on your behalf to Mevr. Jordaan Biedermann Zuider Amstellaan 16, Amsterdam 2. (which name was included in our June list 1942) has been returned owing to the addressee having gone away without leaving a new address. Please advise me to whome we should now re-deliver the parcel.

Yours faithfully,

W. Friedhoff

Second Red Cross letter

21 Dutch Roman Catholic bishops protest against the persecution of the Jews.

## March 1943

1 The 256 residents and staff of a Jewish hospital in Amsterdam for the elderly and disabled deported.
2 First deportation from Westerbork to the new extermination camp at Sobibor.
11 Nazi militia formed.
15 Germans discover that as many as 25,000 Jews may be hidden and institutes a bounty system of seven guilders and fifty cents for each Jew found. This is doubled if the Jew had violated regulations.
22 Working week extended to 54 hours.
23 97% of Dutch physicians strike against Nazi registration.
27 Attempt by resistance group to burn Jewish records at an Amsterdam records office.

## April 1943

10 Jews banned from living in most of the provinces of the Netherlands.
12 Dutch Catholic University at Nijmegen is closed.
16 40 New Zealand bombers attack Haarlem - 85 people killed.
22 Jews banned from living in the remaining provinces of the Netherlands so that all Jews now had to live in Amsterdam, or being in one of the transit camps.
27 Lou Jansen & Jan Dieters leaders of the illegal Dutch political party (CPN) arrested.
30 Strike against forced labour being sent to Germany's war industry.

LONDON COMMITTEE
OF
THE NETHERLAND RED CROSS SOCIETY

PRESIDENT: H. R. H. PRINCESS JULIANA.
VICE PRESIDENT ~~CHAIRMAN:~~ JONKHEER O.C.A. VAN LIDTH DE JEUDE.
CHAIRMAN: BARON HARINXMA.

INFORMATION BUREAU

MRS. R. ALAN LEWIS.
NÉE BARONESS VAN ZUYLEN VAN NYEVELT.

TELEPHONE: ~~GROSVENOR 4101~~,
ABBEY 2117.

120, PALL MALL,
~~STRATTON HOUSE,~~
~~STRATTON STREET,~~
LONDON, ~~W.1.~~
S.W.1.

Gel.ref.aan te halen. 14 Mei 1943
MB.II./h.u.

Mrs.H.Kann,
28 Hemstal Road,
London N.W.6.

Geachte Mevrouw Kann,

Tot mijn leedwezen moet ik U mededeelen dat wij heden dit antwoord ontvangen hebben op het telegram dat wij 16.11.42 voor U verzonden hebben: The Netherland Red Cross in the Hague. "Mrs. JORDAAN-BIEDERMANN is working in Germany since August 1942. No news have been received and her address in unknown." 8.3.43.

Helaas kunnen wij in dit geval niets meer voor U doen, aangezien het Internationale Roode Kruis ons heeft doen weten, dat de Duitschers geen verzoeken om inlichtingen doorlaten, betreffende gedeporteerden. Het Internationale Roode Kruis houdt echter een kaartregister van de gedeporteerden aan, en zodra zij eenig bericht ontvangen over deze personen , zullen wij ons daarvan op de hoogte stellen.

Hoogachtend,
(Maj.) Mary D. de Booy

Red Cross letter in Dutch (see opposite page for translation)

Dear Mrs Kann 14 May 1943

It is with deep regret that I have to advise you that today we received a reply to the telegram sent on your behalf on 16.11.42 to the Netherlands Red Cross in the Hague.

"Mrs JORAAN-BIEDERMANN is working in Germany since August 1942. No news have been received and her address is unknown." 8.3.43.

In this case we are unfortunately not able to do anything more for you, as the International Red Cross has informed us that the Germans do not respond to enquiries for information about deportees. However the International Red Cross does maintain a card index of deportees and as soon as we receive any news about this person we will notify you.

Yours faithfully
(Maj.) Mary de Boog

---

MAY 1943

3 Strike against obligatory labour camps ends after 200 people killed.
7 Dutch men between the ages of 18 to 35 obliged to report to labour camps.
26 Jews riot against Germany in Amsterdam.

JUNE 1943

18 Twelve of the resistance fighters involved in the arson attempt at the records office in March 1943 sentenced to death by the SS.
20 Germans round up more Jews in Amsterdam.
23 Dutch artisans protest against Nazis.
25 Seyss-Inquart orders mass arrest of physicians.

Dr. Hans KLEE

Genf, den 9.Juli 1943.
129, rue de Lausanne.

Frau
Hanna Mann - Crost
London.

Sehr geehrte, gnädige Frau,

nachdem ich seit sehr langer Zeit keine Nachrichten mehr von Ihnen erhalten habe, möchte ich Ihnen diejenigen Briefe, die ich Ihrer Mutter nicht mehr zustellen konnte, wieder zurücksenden, damit Sie sehen, welche Briefe sie nicht mehr erhalten hat. Es sind dies Ihre Schreiben vom 29.10., 5.11. und 12.11. Ferner kam der Brief vom 22.10. zurück, in diesem Falle schicke ich Ihnen auch das Couvert mit, mit dem ich ihn zurückerhalten habe. Schliesslich erhielt ich die anliegenden 3 Bilder, und da ich nicht weiss, von wem sie sonst sein könnten, nehme ich an, es handelt sich um Familien - bilder von Ihnen, die ich Ihnen gleichfalls beifüge.

Ich glaube mich zu erinnern, dass ich damals noch eine andere Sendung Fotos, direkt vom Fotografen[x] erhielt, ohne dass ich natürlich sagen kann, ob diese Bilder, die ich natürlich sofort weiter geschickt habe, Frau Jordan erreicht haben.

Die letzte Nachricht für Sie kam mit dem Absender "W.Mann, B.18, Hooghalen -Oost, Drente", wo das bekannte Internierungslager ist. Etwa um die gleiche Zeit erhielt ich eine Nachricht meiner Eltern, dass Frau Jordan leider nicht mehr in Amsterdam sei und sie mir Mitteilung machen würden, sobald sie eine neue Adresse besässen. Ich fragte dann noch mehrmals an, weil ich doch gerne die noch bei mir liegenden Briefe übermittelt hätte, erhielt jedoch immer den gleichen negativen Bescheid.

Nun habe ich jetzt kaum noch eine Hoffnung, Ihnen behilflich sein zu können, bleibe aber natürlich zu Ihrer Verfügung, wenn Sie etwa durch das Rote Kreuz oder dgl. eine Nachricht erhalten, auf die hin Sie meinen, dass ich etwas für Sie tun kann.

Mit besten Empfehlungen.

Klee.

x Messrs Wallace, Heaton
127 New Bondstreet.

Letter from Dr Klee in Geneva

Dear Mrs Kann

As I have not received any news from you for a while I would like to return to you those letters that I could not forward on to your mother and those that were returned so you can see those which she did not receive. These are your letters of 29.10, 5.11 and 12.11. Furthermore I am also enclosing the letter dated 22.10, together with the envelope, which was returned. Finally I have three photographs and as I do not know from who else they could be I assume that they must be pictures of your family which I also enclose.

As I recall I believe that a while ago I received some photographs directly from the photographer* which I naturally forwarded to Mrs Jordan but do not know if she received them.

The last message received for her showed the senders address as "W. Kann, B18, Hooghalen - Ost, Drente" which is the well known internment camp. At about the same time I received news from my parents that unfortunately Mrs Jordan was no longer in Amsterdam and that they would let me know immediately her new address as soon as they had this information. I enquired of them several times as I would have liked to forward the letters for her in my keeping but each time there was the same negative reply.

Now I have almost no hope of being of any further assistance to you but naturally am at your disposal should you receive news from the Red Cross or from another source and think that I might be of service to you in doing something on your behalf.

Respectfully

*Klee*

** Messrs Wallace, Heaton*
*127 New Bond Street*

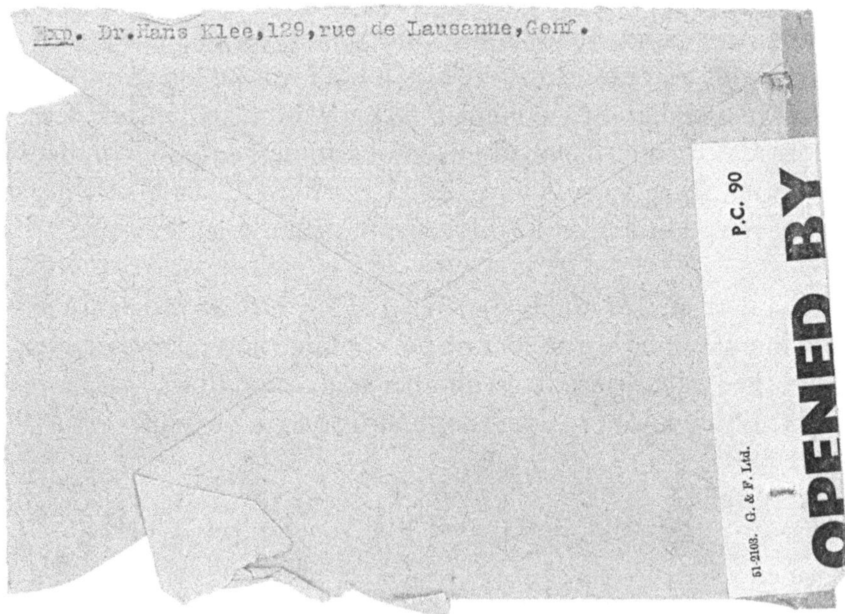


As mentioned earlier all post was subject to censorship as shown by these envelopes.

JULY 1943

6 Children now deported from Westerbork to Sobibor.

SEPTEMBER 1943

29 Last major round up of 5,000 Jews, including Jewish Council leaders, sent to Westerbork.

NOVEMBER 1943

19 'Hollandsche Schouwburg' closed as last group of Jews that had been in hiding had been arrested and deported.

19 First transport from Westerbork to Theresienstadt.

DECEMBER 1943

During this month a start is made for the children of one Jewish parent and a non Jewish parent to be deported so that the Jewish problem can now be totally resolved.

JANUARY 1944

11 First transport from Westerbork for concentration camp Bergen-Belsen.

MAY 1944

1 A second identity card (TD) is introduced to control the issue of ration cards so that members of the resistance and Jews in hiding could not procure food and if doing so would be caught and detained.

JUNE 1944

2 Last deportation from camp Vught to Auschwitz- Vught camp closed down.

5 Allies occupy French beaches - D-Day.

8 Resistance fighter Frans Duwaer arrested.

11 Surprise attack on Arnhem Dome jail by KP gang.

### July 1944

14 Attempt to liberate Jewish prisoners in Amsterdam fails.

20 Plot led by German Claus Von Stauffenberg to kill Hitler fails.

### August 1944

2 Amsterdam soccer team play in orange shirts as a sign of resistance (an oblique reference to the Royal Dutch House of Orange).

9 Twelve workers of Dutch illegal newspaper 'Trouw' executed at camp Vught.

15 Allied air raid on a train in north Netherlands kills 32 people.

18 Allied air raid on Maastricht kills over 80 people.

### September 1944

3 The last of 97 transports from Westerbork leaves for Auschwitz.

4 2,087 Jews sent from Westerbork to Lower Theresienstadt.

5 Known as 'Mad Tuesday' 65,000 Nazi collaborators flee to Germany.

5 Belgium, Netherlands and Luxembourg sign a unity treaty, hence we get the Benelux.

5 Dutch armed forces are formed under Prince Bernhard.

7 Strongest hurricane in over a century hits the Netherlands.

13 Last (99th) deportation from Westerbork of 279 people to Bergen Belsen.

17 Railway strike starts against German occupiers to support Allied troops trying to free the rest of the Netherlands (Arnhem and Operation Market Garden).

20 Nijmegen liberated from German occupation.

27 Helmond and Oss liberated.

30 Dutch form miners union (ABWM).

## October 1944

5 Kerkade liberated.
7 Allies bomb sea dykes near Vlissingen.
7 Riots in Amersfoort, Utrecht and Strugle.
9 Germans turn off electricity in Amsterdam.
11 Allies bomb sea wall at Veere.
21 Canadian troops occupy Breskens.
25 Gas turned off in Amsterdam by German occupiers.
27 Den Bosch and Tilburg freed from Nazi occupation.
30 Scots Highlanders liberate Waalwijk.

## November 1944

1 Zeeland and Flanders liberated.
1 British troops land at Walcheren.
3 Allied commandos land at Westkapelle, Walcheren.
3 German troops in Vlissingen, Walcheren, surrender.
5 Allied troops reach Zoutelande, Walcheren.
8 Last German troops on Walcheren island surrender.
20 Vondelpark in Amsterdam closed because of trees being cut down (for fuel).
20 In Breda Prince Bernhard establishes forces staff.
28 400 people in Rotterdam try to take over a coal storage facility.
28 As a reprisal 40 Dutch men are executed by the Germans.

## December 1944

1 Normal postal deliveries resume in the freed part of south Netherlands.
4 Germans destroy Rhine dykes and flood Betuwe.
5 Germans steal all the silver coinage in Utrecht.
10 9 Dutch citizens hanged by the Nazis.
14 Germans forbid use of electricity in more parts of the Netherlands.
18 German occupiers destroy Amsterdam electricity works.
23 A very harsh winter begins.

### January 1945

4 Germans execute resistance fighters in Amsterdam.
15 Every person in Amsterdam is rationed to 3 kilograms of sugar beet for food.
23 Dutch Premier Gerbrandy tenders his resignation in London.
27 Germans forbid the transport of food to the west of the Netherlands.

### February 1945

23 Gerbrandy forms second administration in London.

### March 1945

3 511 people killed in The Hague due to RAF error when bombing.
3 Roermond and Venlo liberated.
5 RAF bomb The Hague again.
7 SS Police Chief Hans Rauter injured when his car is attacked by Dutch resistance.
8 53 inhabitants of Amsterdam executed by Nazi occupiers.
12 30 more Amsterdam inhabitants executed by Nazi occupiers.
13 Queen Wilhelmina returns to the Netherlands.
31 10 political prisoners are murdered by SS in Zutphen prison.

### April 1945

3 Henglo liberated from Nazi control by Canadian Army.
5 Almelo freed.
8 Nazi General Christiansen flees Netherlands.
10 Canadians take town of Deventer.
14 Arnhem and Zwolle freed from Nazis.
16 Nazi troops in Groningen surrender.
17 German occupiers flood Wieringermeer polder.

20 Germans flood the Beemster and Fencer polders.
25 British troops reach ancient defensive Grebbe Line.
29 RAF drop first food parcels in the Netherlands (Operation Manna).

May 1945

1 Seys-Inquart flees to Flensburg in Germany.
4 German troops in the Netherlands surrender.
5 The Netherlands almost finally liberated by the Canadian Army.
7 SS troops open fire in Amsterdam killing 22 people.
8 European War ends with VE Day.

---

September 1942

16 Hanna's mother age 56 murdered in Auschwitz Extermination Camp

# PARTING THOUGHTS

HOWEVER THIS IS NOT THE END OF THE STORY for those who returned and experienced the horrors at the hands of the Germans and their willing helpers. It continues with the people who survived and who had to cope with being alive when so many had suffered and were dead. For those who had lost parents, siblings, cousins and their extended family being alone was very difficult. Who could they turn to? Who could they tell? Who was interested enough to listen? For most people the war was over and the horrors had finished happening. Life, although very hard, was again in a time of peace. One could look forward to improvement in physical terms as the rebuilding after the war began, but that was not enough for some.

Those that had survived asked "Why me? Why am I here when so many of mine are not? What did I do to deserve to survive?" These were some of the questions which remained and were usually not asked or else pushed to the back of the mind to be stored and ignored. Nobody wanted to know anything and these poor people went into denial. Not only they but also their children who had a very limited family, if any, did not know the reason for their circumstances as the parents never spoke about the past.

The situation of none wanting to know or listen remained in Israel as in the rest of the world. In 1960 with the capture of Adolf

Eichmann and the subsequent trial those not personally touched by the Holocaust began to listen. Then many of those who had locked in their experiences gradually felt able to set them free. In other countries this did not happen until survivors slowly began to relate to others what had happened to them forty or fifty years before, often at a time when they had reached old age. It was as if the telling of their experience was a necessary unburdening before they had to depart this world. But this did not apply to all as some never lived long enough to be able to find release.

It may take some time for the children of those families who survived the terrible events of the 1940s to piece together what happened from what they learn. A following generation may be far enough away not to have an emotional attachment or involvement. For them, or their children, it will become history. But as all events in history if you are not personally involved they just become distant academic facts.

# INDEX OF FOOTNOTES

AH - Adolf Hitler.

Assen - the capital town of the northern Dutch province of Drente.

Biedermeier bonnet - very popular ladies headwear in the 19th century and is a straw bonnet with a wide front rim which has a tying ribbon at the base of the raised part.

(The) Dutch pound is half a kilo or 500 grams so that in fact the weight is just under seven and three quarter English pounds.

Eefke - Bertha's niece, a sibling of Tini, Lini and Ben.

Friedrich Froebel school - a school based on his ideas which offered a holistic kindergarten and primary curriculum led by children's interests.

Gina - Sem's young daughter.

Grete - the sister of Hans and Erich.

High Holidays - the period of Jewish festivals starting at the New Year and lasting several weeks, usually about September/October time.

(Oom) Ies - Bertha's brother and the father to Sem and Myra.

Jacky was exactly a week older than Ray and both grew up to be lifelong friends.

(The) Jewish New Year - this generally falls in September and is part of the High Holidays. It was then a two day celebration.

Jo - married to Lini, one of Hanna's cousins. Jo's brother had worked in London since 1917.

Jordaan - Bertha having taken the name of her second husband.

Karel - another brother of Bertha.

Kinny - married to Bertha's nephew Sem.

Letters - it is a Dutch custom to make or buy confectionary or chocolate in the form of the initial letter of a person's name for their birthday, Christmas or other special occasion.

List - a list of goods that were permitted to be sent to England.

Little shoe - rather than hanging up a stocking on Christmas Eve the Dutch custom allows young children to leave one of their shoes near the fireplace before going to bed. If they are lucky Sint Nicholas may have visited their home during the night and they may find a small present in their shoe in the morning. This happens in the days leading up to the arrival of Sint Nicholas and Black Pieter from Spain on 5th December, the Eve of the Saint's Day. The festival is celebrated more than Christmas Day itself.

Jul - one of Bertha's brothers.

Moeke - common Dutch term of endearment for mother - "mummy".

Myra - Hanna's married cousin living in London.

Next Friday 20/11 - there seems to be a dating oversight as the letter is dated 28/11/41.

Oma - this Oma (grandmother) is the mother of Erich and Hans who is living in Germany and mentions her daughter, son-in-law and granddaughter.

Oom Issy - one of Bertha's brothers.

Opoe/Oome were both nicknames of Bertha's second husband.

Regina (Tante) - wife of Bertha's brother Isaac.

Rosine - Bertha's niece's Eefke's young daughter.

Rosine (Tante) - sister-in-law of Bertha and mother of Tini, Eefke, Lini and Ben.

Speculaas - a popular Dutch spiced biscuit, often in the shape of a windmill.

Therese - one of Bertha's sisters.

Wally - Hans's wife who was living in the Netherlands at that time with their son Gunter.

Yom Kippur - the Day of Atonement, the holiest day in the Jewish calendar marked with a 25 hour fast occurring during the High Holidays.

Yomtov - a Jewish greeting used on festivals meaning have a good day. The Passover festival usually falls in March/April.

Zus - a sister of Kinny and Lex, who all her life liked any excuse to travel somewhere.

www.ingramcontent.com/pod-product-compliance
Ingram Content Group UK Ltd.
Pitfield, Milton Keynes, MK11 3LW, UK
UKHW021522300726
14060UKWH00012B/623

9 781527 216426